THE WORN GARLAND

ALISHA G

INDIA • SINGAPORE • MALAYSIA

ISBN 979-8-89588-907-7

प्रेम गली अति सांकरी, तामें दो न समाई।

To my beloved Krishna,

Tum Ho, Toh Hi Main Hoon!

In a love so pure, that I lose my name,

Like a flame that burns, without a claim.

With every breath of mine, my soul ascends,

To offer it all, and to never end.

My devotion weaves through a silent prayer,

As a bridge to feel You everywhere.

In my longing's ache, and in divine grace,

I find Your love as my solace!

Contents

A Beating Heart

Each morning, just as the sun begins to crest over the temple walls, I make my way through the familiar stone streets. The temple is my sanctuary, my refuge; the stone paths beneath my feet are worn and familiar, but my heart is not as steady. I came not just to offer my prayers, not just to lose myself in the tranquility of the temple's ancient halls; I came for him.

He stands apart from the world - radiant in a way that makes the very air around him feel different. There is something otherworldly about his presence, something that made every whisper of his name, every murmur of his voice, feel like a blessing. People flocked to him, seeking more than just his smile. They sought his very essence, the way his presence seemed to pull at something deep within them. His smile can disarm the most troubled heart. It is no wonder that every person in the town finds a reason to linger a little longer in his presence.

And I, too, find myself drawn to him, though I cannot find the courage to step forward, to tell him this in words.

My eyes seek him daily. I watch him, careful not to let anyone notice how my gaze always lingers on him a little longer than it should. He is so far above me, so unreachable, and yet my heart aches with unspoken words, with a longing I can barely understand. He is a celebrated figure, the kind that people whisper about with reverence and admiration. There is no place for my small, quiet feelings in the midst of that.

Yet, I come. Every day, I come.

The temple courtyard bustles with the usual crowd: devotees seeking blessings, young women lingering with hopeful smiles, and their laughter mingling with the chime of temple bells. I stand at the edge, my fingers gripping the edge of my saree tightly as I watch him. His face is serene, and his presence is divine. I feel a flutter in my chest, the same one I feel every single time I see him. Did he notice me? How could he?

In the sea of faces, I am just one more admirer.

And what if he never looked at me? What if his heart, like everyone else's, was already full of the adoration that followed him wherever he went? I am just a girl - simple, ordinary, unnoticed. What could I offer different from the countless others who vied for his attention?

I stay on the edge of this world, silent, blending into the stone walls, into the garlands of jasmine and marigolds that fill the temple air with fragrance. I cannot afford to let anyone see how I look at him. My friends would surely notice, would tease me endlessly, and worst of all, they may discover my secret.

What would they say if they knew? What will they do if they see my heart laid bare, filled with something I dare not speak aloud? I fear the mockery, the prying questions, but more than that, I fear that my love - so fragile, so small in the vastness of everything he was - may seem foolish to those who can never understand it.

He moved through the temple with a grace that seemed effortless, as if he were a part of the very air, the very light that filtered through the temple pillars. His every gesture was calm, deliberate, and filled with a kind of peace that made people stop and stare. My heart fluttered as I watched him.

The days passed in this quiet ritual - my hidden glances, my silent prayers. I cannot speak about my feelings openly; I cannot let them take form in words. I am too scared, and my feelings are too delicate, like the petals of the flowers I bring to the temple each day. My love, though unspoken, is as constant as the sun that rises each morning to light the temple walls.

And yet, my feet still carry me here each morning, drawn to him by something I cannot name, something too fragile and too precious to speak aloud.

I stay silent, watching, waiting, hoping. I know I am but a small part of the world that swirls around him. And yet, each day, I return to the temple, my heart filled with the same quiet love, the same silent devotion. I ask for nothing and expect nothing, and still, the thought of him lingers with me like a prayer that has no end.

My Father, My Guru

My father, Vishnuchittar, is unlike anyone I've ever known. For as long as I can remember, his life has revolved around his deep love and devotion to Lord Vishnu. He has deep devotion and unwavering faith towards Lord Vishnu. People have huge respect and high regards for him and he is known as Periyalvar, the "Great Alvar".

Everything he does, every action, every word, is an offering to the Lord. He is a gentle, humble soul filled with quiet wisdom that radiates from him in the simplest of ways. His presence brings peace, not only to me but to everyone who comes near him.

He leads a simple life in our small town of Srivilliputhur. He is no scholar of great renown, nor does he seek fame or fortune. His heart is content with offering his love to Lord Vishnu, whom he worships with unwavering devotion. His days are spent tending to our garden, growing the most beautiful flowers to weave into garlands for the Lord. Each petal and each bloom that he touched is filled with his devotion, for to my father, offering a garland to Vishnu is like offering his very soul.

We lived peacefully in Srivilliputhur, with my father's heart firmly rooted in serving the Lord. But the Lord, in His boundless grace, had other plans for him that would soon unfold in a way none of us could have imagined.

Far away in Madurai, the Pandya king, Vallabhadeva, was troubled by a profound question:

Who is the Supreme God, and what is the path to salvation?

The king, though wise and just, could not find a satisfying answer, so he declared a grand assembly in his court. He invited learned scholars and philosophers from across the land to debate and answer his query, promising a great reward and royal honor to whoever could clarify his dilemma.

While the scholars gathered in Madurai, my father remained unaware of the king's quest. He focused on his garlands and prayers, far from the royal debates. But then, something miraculous happened - something that would change everything.

One night, as my father lay asleep, he had a vision - Lord Vishnu Himself appeared to him in a dream. In His infinite kindness, the Lord spoke to my father and told him to go to Madurai and answer the king's question.

"You, Vishnuchittar, must go," the Lord said. *"Go to the court and tell them of Me. Tell them that I, Vishnu, am the Supreme Lord, and Bhakti is the true path to salvation."*

My father, ever humble, was filled with doubt.

"How can I, a simple gardener, stand before kings and scholars? What do I know of royal courts and debates?"

But the Lord smiled and reassured him.

"True knowledge comes not from books, but from the heart. Speak of your love for Me, and all will be well."

With the Lord's blessing, my father set out for Madurai, his heart filled with humility and the resolve to do as the Lord commanded.

When my father arrived in the grand court of Madurai, the air was thick with debate. Scholars and philosophers were engaged in deep discussions, each presenting their theories on the nature of the divine. The court was filled with the finest minds, and amidst them all stood my father - simple, unassuming, with no titles or grand speeches.

When it was his turn to speak, my father did not recite complicated arguments. Instead, he spoke from his heart. He told the king and the court that Lord Vishnu is the Supreme Being, the protector of all, the one who takes countless forms to save His devotees. He spoke of the Lord's *avatars* - Rama, Krishna, and the others - and how they had come to restore dharma on Earth. Most of all, he spoke of *Bhakti* - the path of love and devotion as the truest way to reach the Lord.

As my father spoke, the court fell silent, not because his words were learned or scholarly but because they were filled with devotion that transcended intellect. His love for Vishnu shone through every word, and even the learned scholars could feel the depth of his faith.

The king, deeply moved, declared my father the victor of the assembly. He recognized that the simple devotion in my father's heart was far greater than any philosophical argument. To honor him, the king ordered that my father be paraded through the streets of Madurai on the royal elephant - a gesture reserved only for the greatest of men.

But it was during this grand procession that something even more extraordinary occurred. As my father was paraded through the streets, suddenly, in the sky, Lord Vishnu Himself appeared, seated majestically on Garuda, with Goddess Lakshmi by His side. My father's eyes filled with tears as he beheld the divine vision, overwhelmed by the Lord's grace.

Yet, in that moment of divine glory, my father did something that still fills my heart with awe. Instead of basking in the honor and blessings being showered upon him, he was overcome with concern for the Lord. He thought,

How can I, a mere mortal, gaze upon the Lord? What if some evil force tries to harm Him?

And so, from the depths of his heart, my father began to sing verses of protection for Lord Vishnu.

He sang the famous *Pallandu* - a prayer for the Lord's safety:

pallāṇḍu pallāṇḍu pallāyirattāṇḍu

pala kōḍi nūṟāyiram

mallāṇḍa tiṇḍōl maṇivaṇṇā !

un śēvaḍi śevvi tirukkāppu

Many years! Many years! Thousands of years!

Many crores, hundreds of thousands of years!

O Lord with the hue of a gem, who defeated the mighty wrestlers!

May your red lotus feet be forever safe!

In his immense love for the Lord, my father sang as though the all-powerful Vishnu needed his protection. It was a beautiful expression of his devotion - *a reversal of roles, where the devotee sought to protect the protector.*

This act of love and humility touched everyone who witnessed it, including the king. From that day on, my father was no longer known as Vishnuchittar. He became Periyalvar - the "Great Alvar," for his devotion was unmatched, his love so pure that he sang for the Lord's well-being.

The king honored him greatly, but my father's heart remained humble. He returned to Srivilliputhur to his simple life of weaving garlands for the Lord. Yet, the "Pallandu" he sang that day continued to echo through the ages, sung in temples all across the land as a prelude to the daily worship of Lord Ranganatha.

As I reflect on my father's journey, I feel blessed to have been raised by such a soul. His devotion has guided my path, and I see in him the perfect example of love for the Lord. His victory in Madurai was not one of intellect or scholarship but of devotion.

I've grown up watching him tend to the sacred *Tulsi* garden that surrounds our home, day after day, with love so deep it feels like he is caring for the plants as though they are extensions of Lord Ranganatha himself. The garden is his sanctuary, and he treats every leaf and flower with the utmost reverence. To him, each living being is a divine gift, a way to connect to the Lord. When he waters the plants or picks flowers for garlands, I see how his heart and mind constantly focus on the Lord, as if there is no separation between his daily tasks and his worship.

My father speaks a few words, but his silence is never empty. It's filled with the presence of Vishnu as if he is in constant communion with the divine. He doesn't need to speak for me to understand the depth of his devotion - his entire being reflects it. His love for the Lord isn't confined to rituals or prayers; it's woven into everything he does. When he prays, it's as though time stops and the world becomes still, just listening to the sincerity of his devotion. His hymns to Narayana are not just words - they are his heart laid bare.

As a father, he has shown me nothing but love, but it's a love that's intertwined with something more significant. I've learned so much from him, not just through his teachings but by watching how he lives his life, with every breath dedicated to the Lord.

My father never seeks recognition or praise for his devotion. In fact, he shies away from such things. He is content in his humble life, knowing that everything he does is for Vishnu, which is enough for him. Though he has such profound knowledge of the scriptures, he never boasts. Instead, he lives, quietly, constantly reminding me that true devotion comes from the heart, not from outward displays.

Growing up in his presence has shaped me more than I can express. I see in him the kind of devotion I aspire to - the kind that doesn't need to be spoken, because it is lived. He has taught me that serving Narayana is not just about offering prayers or hymns; it's about offering yourself in every moment.

My Childhood

My childhood home is simple but sacred, a place where every corner and room seems to echo with the love and devotion my father and I share for Lord Vishnu. Our house is small, built with humble materials, but to me, it feels like a temple. It isn't the size or grandeur that matters - it's the atmosphere of devotion that fills the space. Every breath of air inside feels like a prayer, every beam of light a blessing from the Lord.

The heart of our home is the *Tulsi* garden, or *Tulsi Vanam*, as we call it. This sacred space isn't just a garden - it's the soul of our household. My father tends to the plants with such care, and I spend countless hours there, plucking flowers, weaving garlands, and offering them to Vishnu. The scent of *Tulsi* fills the air, mingling with the fragrance of jasmine and roses, creating an atmosphere that always feels serene, as if the Lord Himself is present among the plants.

Inside the house, we have a small altar dedicated to Narayana. It isn't grand or ornate, but it is the most sacred space in our home. My father and I rise early every morning to light the lamps and offer prayers. The flickering light of the lamps, combined with the soft chants of my father's hymns, fills the house with a divine warmth.

Though our home is modest, my father ensures that my upbringing is rich in spiritual knowledge and love. He teaches me how to recite prayers, sing hymns, and, most importantly, live a life dedicated to Ranganatha. We don't have much material wealth, but I never feel lacking. In fact,

I always feel blessed, surrounded by my father's love and Vishnu's presence in every aspect of our lives.

There are no grand halls or opulent decorations in our home, but what we have is precious - my father's wisdom, his love, and his devotion to the Lord. The walls of our home are made of clay, simple and robust, but they feel like they are made of something more sacred. I grew up hearing my father's voice softly echo through those walls as he sang his praises to Vishnu. Even the most mundane parts of our home - the kitchen, where we prepare food offerings for the Lord, and the courtyard, where we sit and speak of the divine - feel blessed. To me, it isn't just a house; it is a living embodiment of devotion.

My father keeps a few sacred texts, which are worn with time but treated with the utmost respect. He often sits with me in the evenings, reading aloud the stories of Vishnu's *avatars*, his voice filled with reverence. The stories of Krishna and Rama fill my heart with joy, and as I listen to him, I feel as though the Lord is speaking directly to me through my father's words.

Our home is a place where the divine resides. Every morning, the light of the rising sun filters through the windows, and as it touches the *Tulsi* plants and the altar, I feel a deep sense of gratitude that I am being raised in such a sacred space.

The Joy of Devotion

I kneel before you, Lord Vishnu, my hands folded and my forehead resting lightly on the cool stone of the temple floor. As I close my eyes, the world outside fades away, and all I can feel is your presence, surrounding me like a gentle embrace. *You are always near, aren't you?*

I feel your closeness in every moment of my life. Even when my friends are off playing games or running through the fields, I find myself drawn to the temple, to the quiet stillness of prayer. I know my childhood is not like theirs. While they find joy in chasing each other and laughing in the sun, my heart longs for something else - something more profound. I find my happiness in the peaceful silence of devotion, in the offering of flowers, and in the soft hum of hymns sung in your honor.

While others play and laugh, my heart finds joy in prayer, in the quiet whisper of devotion, where I feel you the most, O Narayana.

I love to be with my friends, but even when I am with them, there's a part of me that is always thinking of you. When they ask me to play hide and seek, I join them, but my mind often drifts to the temple, imagining myself kneeling before you, offering my prayers. It's not that I don't enjoy playing, but I find a different kind of happiness in prayer. While others seek fun, I seek the peace that comes from being close to you. I feel that my purpose is more than play, more than just running through the fields.

Something inside me calls me toward you, O Narayana, and pulls me to serve you and live for a greater purpose.

My father notices this difference in me, though he doesn't say much about it. He understands, I think. He sees how, while other children run and chase, I prefer to sit with him in the garden, picking flowers for your garlands. While picking flowers, I feel His presence more than anywhere else. Every petal we pick, every garland we weave, is for Him. He tells me stories of your greatness as we work, and I listen with my heart wide open, soaking in every word. I feel more at peace in these moments, surrounded by the quiet beauty of nature, knowing that everything we do is for you.

Even in my everyday tasks, I feel this sense of higher purpose. While my friends may grow restless with household chores, I find peace in them. Whether sweeping the floor, helping my father with cooking, or carrying water from the well, these small acts of service give me immense happiness. I offer each task as though it is part of my devotion and the life I want to live in your name. Each small chore is a way of serving not just those around me but serving him, and that gives me a sense of peace and fulfillment that nothing else can.

Sometimes, I see the other children laughing, and for a moment, I wonder what it would be like to be like them - to live a life without this deep sense of devotion, to spend my days carefree, thinking only of the games we play. But that thought passes quickly because I know I wouldn't trade this feeling in my heart for anything. The peace I feel in prayer, the joy I find in offering my devotion to you, is far greater than anything else. I may not be like the others, but that's alright. I feel called to something higher that fills me with purpose beyond the ordinary.

My friends sometimes ask me why I spend so much time in the temple and don't play as much as they do. I smile and tell them that I find joy in different things. They may not understand, but that's okay. I know that what I feel is real - that this devotion and calling come from deep within. I think a purpose that goes beyond the games, beyond the everyday. I feel that I am meant to serve, to live for something greater than myself.

My childhood is different, but it is full of joy - the quiet joy that comes from knowing that I am living for something higher and more significant than myself. And in that, I find peace.

A Day in My Life

The daily ritual of dressing Him had become more than just a sacred duty. It was our time together, our playful moments when He, in His own divine way, would tease me, as if to remind me that He wasn't just a distant deity but a companion who shared in my love, my joy, and my mischief.

I enter the puja room with my basket of fresh flowers, jewelry, and His *dhoti.* Today, I had chosen jasmine and roses for His garland - He loves jasmine the most, or so I believed. I kneel before Him, smiling as I imagine what today's ritual might bring. Vishnu's statue stands still, serene as always, but I know better. He isn't just a stone to me. He is alive in spirit, waiting to play our little game.

Good morning, O Narayana, I whisper softly, looking up at His gentle face. As I begin to prepare His *dhoti*, something happens that makes me chuckle softly to myself - the fabric slips from my hands, falling to the floor. I bent down to pick it up, only to feel as though a soft breeze had caused it to flutter from my grip again.

Oh, my Lord, are You teasing me already? I ask playfully, looking up at His smiling face. I can almost hear His laughter in the rustling leaves outside.

I pick up the *dhoti* once more and it falls again. I understood today, he is in a mood to wear cyan color *dhoti* and not the orange one. I take the cyan *dhoti* start wrapping it carefully around Him. This time, it stays in place, but I can feel His presence, watching me, waiting for His next move.

As I reach for the gold chain I had chosen for Him today, it slips through my fingers, clinking to the floor with a soft sound. I sigh, though inside, my heart was full of joy. This is a part of our game.

Is this Your doing again? I ask, shaking my head with a smile. *Are You testing my patience?*

I lean down to pick it up, but just as I am about to place the necklace around His neck, it slips again, falling back into my lap. I cannot help but laugh. *So, You want to play today, don't You?* I say, my voice full of affection. *Very well, I will play along.*

With a determined smile, I hold the necklace firmly this time, finally managing to fasten it around His neck. As I do so, I feel the warmth of His presence, like a gentle embrace. He is here, with me, playing His sweet little games to remind me that love doesn't always have to be serious - it can be playful, too.

Next comes His bracelets. I had just slid one onto His wrist when I notice that the other had mysteriously disappeared from the small box where I usually keep His jewelry. I frown, looking around the temple floor, but the bracelet is nowhere to be seen.

You've hidden it, haven't You? I ask, half-amused, half-exasperated. *You like to make me work for it, don't You?*

I looked under the altar, near the flowers, and finally find it nestled among the petals. I shake my head, laughing softly. *You can't hide from me. I will always find You.*

As I place the bracelet on His wrist, I feel a sense of accomplishment, as though I had won our little game. But of course, Vishnu is yet to play more. I am trying to put the flower garland around His neck, and here he is playing His favorite trick. The garland slips from my fingers not once, not twice, but three times, each time landing softly at His feet.

You are impossible! I laugh, though my heart was bursting with love. *But I won't give up so easily.*

Finally, with a firm grip, I lift the garland and carefully place it around His neck, adjusting the flowers so they sit perfectly against His chest. I step back to admire his beauty, and as I do so, I can almost feel His eyes twinkling with mischief, as though He is laughing with me.

There, my Lord. You look perfect, despite all Your tricks, I say with a grin, feeling the warmth of His presence surround me.

But the game isn't over yet. Just as I turn to pick up the flowers to place near his feet, I feel a soft tug on the *dhoti* I had just so carefully arranged. I turned around, and sure enough, a small section had come undone, as though He had playfully pulled it just to see what I would do.

You're relentless today! I exclaim, my heart full of joy. *But I will not let You win, not today!*

With a soft laugh, I fix the *dhoti* once more, this time securing it tightly around Him. Finally, I place the flowers around His feet.

Now, You are ready, I whisper, looking up at Him with all the love in my heart. *But only because I am persistent, my Lord!*

I step back to admire Him, my beloved Vishnu, now adorned in the clothes, jewelry, and flowers I had so lovingly offered. Despite His playful tricks, I had succeeded in dressing Him perfectly, just as I did every morning. But it wasn't about perfection - it was about the connection, the game we played, the love that filled every moment of our time together.

As I leave the puja room, I can still feel His presence, his mischievous energy lingering in the air. My heart feels light, filled with the love we shared, and I know that tomorrow, He would tease me again, dropping jewels, loosening His *dhoti*, playing with me just as He always did.

The Divine Flame

Every day, I light a small lamp before Vishnu's image, a simple flame to keep His presence alive in my home. The flicker of the flame has always brought me comfort, a reminder that even in the stillness of my surroundings, He is here with me. As I sit in prayer, I watch the flame dance and sway, and at times, it feels as though it is more than just fire - it feels alive, as if it shares in the devotion I offer to Him.

I've often noticed the way the flame responds to my prayers. Sometimes, when I am deep in thought, offering my heart to Vishnu, the flame flickers gently, as though it is listening. And there are moments, rare and precious, when it brightens suddenly, glowing with an intensity that takes me by surprise. It's in those moments that I feel closest to Him, as though the flame itself is carrying my love to Him across the realms.

Tonight, after a long session of prayer, something extraordinary happens. As I sit before His image, the room filled with the soft hum of my whispered prayers, I notice the flame begin to change. It grows brighter, larger, filling the entire room with a golden glow. I blink, unsure if my eyes are playing tricks on me, but the light continues to grow, soft and radiant, as though the flame is no longer just a small lamp but a beacon of something divine.

I feel my heart quicken. There's a warmth in the room now, not just from the fire, but from something more - something that feels like His presence. I can't explain it, but I know that Vishnu is here. The flame isn't just light anymore; it feels like an extension of Him, a symbol of the divine connection between us. It flickers softly, bending slightly toward me, as if bowing in acknowledgment of my love and devotion.

My breath catches, and I feel tears welling up in my eyes - not from sorrow, but from the overwhelming joy of knowing that He is with me. The flame's glow wraps around me, filling the space with a sacred warmth, and in that moment, I am certain that He is watching, that He sees me. This isn't just fire. This is His light, His love, reaching out to touch my soul.

I sit in silence, my heart overflowing with gratitude, as the flame continues to burn brightly, casting golden light across the room. I feel as though time has stopped, and all that exists is this moment - this beautiful, miraculous moment where Vishnu and I are connected through the light. The room feels sacred, transformed by the divine presence that fills it.

As the flame flickers again, its glow softer now, I feel an unspoken assurance deep within me. This is more than a simple lamp; this is a sign. A sign that He is always near, that my prayers are heard, that my love is returned. The flame, radiant and pure, is a symbol of the bond between us, a bond that transcends this world, a bond that burns as brightly as the light before me.

Even as the flame begins to settle, its glow dimming slightly, the warmth in my heart remains. I know now, more than ever, that Vishnu is always with me, responding to my devotion in ways both subtle and profound. The flame, once a simple lamp, has become a reminder of His love, His presence, and the unbreakable connection between our souls.

The Melodious Notes

The evening air is cool and still, as the soft golden light of the setting sun wraps around everything like a warm embrace. I sit beneath the broad *peepal* tree, its leaves gently swaying in the breeze. The world around me is serene, bathed in the colors of twilight - pinks and oranges fading into a deep blue sky, soon to welcome the stars. The earth feels alive beneath me, a sense of calm settling into the land as if nature itself is preparing for a peaceful night.

I sit there in stillness, my mind at ease. There is no restlessness in my heart, just a quiet contentment as I enjoy the beauty of the moment. The simple red saree I wear, with its delicate gold border, moves softly with the wind. A *Tulsi* garland hangs around my neck, its scent mingling with the jasmine flowers braided into my hair. It's a peaceful evening, much like many others I've spent beneath this tree, where I often find solace and stillness. I am not waiting for anything, just sitting in the embrace of nature, feeling connected to everything around me.

And then, without any warning, a sound begins to drift through the air. It's faint at first, so soft I wonder if it's the wind playing tricks on me. But as I listen closer, I realize it's a melody - a flute, its sweet notes curling through the breeze like a delicate thread pulling me toward something divine. The music is soft and entrancing, and though it is unexpected, it feels as if it belongs in this moment, as natural as the rustling of the leaves or the distant hum of insects in the fields.

The melody grows clearer, and with it comes a warmth, a sense of familiarity. I don't know where it's coming from, but I don't question it. The music is so pure, so beautiful, that I close my eyes and simply listen. The world around me seems to soften as the flute's melody fills the air, and I find myself being drawn into something beyond the present, beyond the world as I know it.

When I open my eyes, I'm no longer beneath the peepal tree. Instead, I am in a place that feels like a dream - a lush, green landscape filled with blooming flowers, their colors more vibrant than I've ever seen. The air is fragrant with the scent of jasmine and sandalwood, and the sky above is a deep, rich blue, as though twilight has paused, waiting for something divine. Everything around me feels alive, as if the land itself is filled with divine energy.

And then I see Him.

Standing beneath a grand *Kadamba* tree, my beloved Vishnu appears before me in His form as Krishna, playing His flute. His golden - yellow silk garments shimmer in the soft light, and a peacock feather rests in His hair, gently swaying as He plays. His eyes are closed, completely absorbed in the music He creates, and His skin glows like the night sky, dark and radiant. The melody flows from His flute, and as I watch Him, my heart swells with a sense of peace, joy, and love that I have never known.

I stand there, simply watching, not needing to move or speak. The music is all around me, filling every corner of my being with a blissful calm. There's no rush, no urgency - just the pure, divine connection that exists between us. The world around us feels like it's celebrating this moment. Flowers bloom more brightly, and the air hums with a gentle energy, as if even nature itself is aware of the miracle unfolding.

Celestial beings appear, their forms glowing softly in the distance, showering petals of lotus and jasmine upon us. The sky above twinkles with soft lights, not quite stars, but something more divine, as if the heavens have opened to witness this sacred moment. The sound of the flute fills the air, and I feel as though I am no longer standing still - I am part of the music, part of the divine rhythm that flows from Him.

The world around us seems to breathe with every note He plays, and in those moments, there is no distinction between me and Him. It's as if the universe itself has orchestrated this meeting, this union, where I feel the deepest connection to Vishnu - not through words or prayers, but through this melody that carries His love directly to my heart.

Then, slowly, the music begins to fade, its final notes lingering in the air like a soft whisper. Vishnu opens His eyes and meets my gaze. His smile is gentle, filled with love, and it tells me everything I need to know - that this was not a dream, but a divine gift. I feel the peace settle into my heart, knowing that this moment, this natural miracle, was

His way of showing me that He is always present, always near.

Before I can take another step, the world around me begins to shift, the colors and sounds softening. The lush greenery, the flowers, the celestial beings - all begin to dissolve, and I find myself back beneath the peepal tree, the evening air still and quiet around me. But the sound of the flute remains, echoing in my heart, a reminder of the divine connection I had just experienced.

I sit there, smiling to myself, knowing that what I felt was real. It was not something I sought, but something that came naturally, a beautiful reminder of the bond between my soul and my beloved Vishnu. The flute's melody lingers in the air, and I know that wherever I go, that music will always be with me, a gentle sign of His love.

Dasavatar – The Ten Incarnations

My father's voice was my greatest source of joy in my early years. Every evening, as the day softened into dusk, he would gather me on his lap and weave stories that felt like they were carried on the wind from some far-off divine land. My favorite stories were always of Vishnu, the Preserver, and his *avatars*. I was fascinated, captivated, even by the idea that the Lord himself would descend into the world to protect it.

My father would recount each *avatar* in vivid detail, his voice rich with reverence and awe. The way he spoke of Vishnu, Rama's unwavering righteousness, and Krishna's playful wisdom made the tales come alive. I would sit there, wide-eyed, imagining each moment - the ocean churning as Kurma supported the world, the moment when Narasimha tore through Hiranyakashipu, or the tender moments when Krishna would steal butter, all to teach the world about divine love.

Every story deepened my yearning to be closer to this divine force that moved through our world in countless forms. I used to meditate on each *avatar* and ask for the stories to be narrated repeatedly.

Matsya (Fish *Avatar*)

The Matsya *avatar* is Lord Vishnu's first incarnation, where He appeared as a great fish. In this form, the Lord saved the sacred Vedas and the seeds of life from a massive deluge that threatened to engulf the world. As the flood waters rose to cover the Earth, Vishnu, as Matsya, guided the boat carrying the seven great sages (Saptarishi) and the seeds of all living creatures to safety. This *avatar* symbolizes the protection of knowledge and the preservation of life during times of great destruction.

Listening to the story of Matsya, my heart fills with gratitude for the Lord's infinite compassion. How amazing that He would take the humble form of a fish to protect the knowledge of the universe! It shows me that the Lord is always watching over us, ensuring that knowledge, wisdom, and life itself will be preserved even in the darkest times. I see in this *avatar* a reminder of the Lord's care for His devotees, no matter how small or insignificant they may feel. Even when the world is drowning in chaos, I trust that Lord Vishnu will guide me, just as He guided the boat through the floods, protecting me and leading me toward salvation.

Kurma (Tortoise *Avatar*)

In His second incarnation, Lord Vishnu took the form of Kurma, the giant tortoise, to support the churning of the cosmic ocean (*Samudra Manthan*). The gods and demons had come together to churn the ocean to extract *amrita* (the nectar of immortality), using Mount Mandara as the churning rod. However, the mountain began to sink into the ocean under its weight. In this crucial moment, in the form of Kurma, Vishnu supported the mountain on His back, allowing the churning to continue and ensuring that the nectar was obtained.

The image of Lord Vishnu as Kurma, patiently holding up the great mountain on His back, reminds me of His silent strength and willingness to carry the world's burdens. The Lord is not only our protector but also our supporter in times of need. Just as He supported the churning of the ocean, He supports me in my spiritual journey, ensuring that I continue striving for divine nectar, His love and grace. His willingness to bear the weight of the world teaches me that no burden is too heavy for Him, and I am comforted knowing that whenever I feel overwhelmed, He is there, silently carrying me through it.

Varaha (Boar *Avatar*)

In the Varaha *avatar*, Lord Vishnu appeared as a mighty boar to rescue the Earth goddess Bhoomi Devi. The demon Hiranyaksha had kidnapped her and submerged her in the cosmic ocean. Varaha dived into the waters, fought the demon, and lifted the Earth on His tusks, restoring her to her rightful place in the universe. This *avatar* represents the victory of good over evil and the Lord's commitment to protecting the Earth and its inhabitants.

As I listen to the tale of Varaha, my heart is filled with admiration and love for the Lord's heroic act of saving Bhooma Devi. It reminds me that Lord Vishnu will always come to the aid of His devotees, no matter how deep the darkness seems. The image of the Lord lifting the Earth from the ocean depths symbolizes how He lifts each of us out of the depths of our struggles and restores us to the light. His love for the Earth, and by extension, for all beings, assures me that I am always under His protection. Varaha's strength and bravery give me the courage to face life's challenges, knowing that the Lord will lift me out of despair, just as He lifted Bhooma Devi.

Narasimha (Man-Lion *Avatar*)

The Narasimha *avatar* is one of the most awe-inspiring forms of Lord Vishnu. To protect His young devotee, Prahlada, from his tyrannical father, Hiranyakashipu, the Lord appeared as Narasimha – half-man and half-lion. Hiranyakashipu had been granted a boon that made him almost impossible to kill. Still, Vishnu, in His Narasimha form, emerged from a pillar at twilight and, using His claws, tore apart the demon in a way that satisfied all the conditions of the boon. This *avatar* represents the Lord's fierce love for His devotees and His ability to manifest in any form necessary to protect them.

Hearing the story of Narasimha fills me with awe and reverence. The Lord's fierce and protective form shows me that He will stop at nothing to protect His devotees, especially those who are pure in heart like Prahlada. Narasimha's terrifying appearance was meant to strike fear into the wicked, yet his gentle embrace of Prahlada afterward reminds me that the Lord is always compassionate to those who love Him. I reflect on how the Lord will manifest in any way, even in the most unexpected forms, to save us. His boundless love, both fierce and tender, reassures me that I, too, am under His constant protection, no matter how great the trials I face.

Vamana (Dwarf *Avatar*)

Vamana, the fifth *avatar* of Vishnu, appeared as a dwarf Brahmin during the reign of the demon king Bali, who had conquered the three worlds. Vamana approached the king and humbly asked for three paces of land. Bali, proud of his power, agreed to the seemingly small request. However, Vamana then expanded to a gigantic form, covering the Earth and the heavens in two strides. With no space left, Bali offered his head for the third step, and Vishnu, pleased by his humility, granted him a place in the netherworld as its ruler. This *avatar* is a testament to the Lord's wisdom and his ability to humble even the most powerful beings.

The story of Vamana is humbling. The Lord's ability to appear in such a small, unassuming form and yet perform such a monumental act reminds me that true greatness lies in humility. Vamana teaches me that it is not the size of our actions that matters but the intention behind them. His transformation into a cosmic form shows the boundless nature of the Lord, who can expand to fill the entire universe or remain present in the smallest of beings. I pray for the humility of Vamana, wishing to approach Lord Ranganatha with a pure heart, knowing that He will always fulfill my deepest spiritual desires with His infinite grace.

Parashurama (Warrior with the Axe)

Lord Vishnu incarnated as Parashurama, a fierce warrior armed with an axe, to rid the Earth of corrupt and oppressive kings. Parashurama was born to a Brahmin family but took up the role of a Kshatriya (warrior) to restore dharma. His wrath was directed at rulers who had abused their power and oppressed their subjects. After fulfilling His mission, Parashurama retired to a life of asceticism, symbolizing the balance between righteous action and renunciation.

The story of Parashurama fills me with a sense of respect for the Lord's commitment to justice. This *avatar* reminds me that dharma must always be upheld and that even the powerful must be held accountable for their actions. Parashurama teaches me that there is a time for action and a time for peace, and that the Lord uses His power not for vengeance but to restore balance and righteousness in the world. I pray for the strength to uphold dharma in my life and to be fearless in the face of injustice, trusting that the Lord will guide my actions toward righteousness, just as He did for Parashurama.

Rama (Prince of Ayodhya)

The seventh incarnation of Vishnu, Lord Rama, is revered as the embodiment of dharma (righteousness) and virtue. His life, as described in the **Ramayana**, is a story of sacrifice, duty, and unwavering adherence to moral principles. Rama faced numerous challenges, including exile from His kingdom, the abduction of His wife Sita by the demon king

Ravana, and the ensuing battle to rescue her. Throughout it all, Rama remained the ideal king, husband, and son, showcasing the values of righteousness and selflessness.

Rama's story touches my heart deeply, for his life represents the perfect example of dharma. His unwavering commitment to his duties, even in the face of great personal loss and suffering, inspires me to live according to the divine principles of righteousness. I think of Sita, his devoted consort, and her enduring love and faith in Rama, and I feel a deep connection to her.

Sita was the daughter of the Earth, born from the furrow when King Janaka was plowing the field, a gift from Bhooma Devi.Sita's love for Lord Rama, devotion to Him, and commitment to standing by Him in all circumstances inspire me deeply. I, too, have spent my life in unwavering love for Lord Vishnu, specifically in His form as Lord Ranganatha. Just as Sita's life was centered on Lord Rama, every moment of my life is centered on Lord Vishnu.

One of the most substantial parallels between Sita and me is our longing for the Lord. Sita's separation from Lord Rama during her time in Lanka mirrors my deep yearning for union with Lord Ranganatha. While Sita's separation was physical, my separation from the Lord is more spiritual, a feeling of distance that drives my every prayer, song, and thought toward Him.

Just as Sita remained unwavering in her love and loyalty to Rama despite being far from Him, I, too, experience that intense longing. Every day, I yearn for Lord Ranganatha to take me as His bride. The *Thiruppavai* hymns I compose are filled with this yearning, just as Sita's heart was filled with thoughts of Rama while in Ashoka Vatika. In both stories, this separation intensifies our devotion, making our love for the Lord all the more powerful.

Sita is the epitome of patience and surrender. Her unwavering faith in Lord Rama during her captivity exemplifies true surrender to the divine. She endured the trials of separation, but she never lost hope or faith. I, too, have surrendered my heart entirely to Lord Ranganatha, trusting in His divine will. Even though I live in the human world, I feel His presence everywhere and know that one day, He will take me into His divine embrace.

Like Sita, I trust the divine timing. Sita patiently waited for Lord Rama's arrival, knowing that he would rescue her and restore her to her rightful place by His side. Similarly, I live each day in joyful anticipation of the day I will be united with Lord Ranganatha, for I know He has heard my prayers and knows the depth of my love for Him.

Sita's marriage to Lord Rama is not just a royal union but a sacred bond between the divine and the devoted soul. Similarly, my desire to marry Lord Ranganatha represents the union between the *Jivatma* (individual soul) and the *Paramatma* (Supreme Soul). Sita embodies the perfect wife, dedicated to her husband in mind, body, and soul, and I see myself as the eternal bride of Vishnu, longing for that divine union.

Both Sita and I represent the ideal of *Pativrata Dharma* - complete devotion to the husband, which symbolizes the soul's devotion to the Supreme Lord. No matter the trials she faced, Sita never wavered in her devotion to Rama. In the same way, I dedicate myself to Lord Vishnu, seeking to live up to the ideals of divine love and service.

Sita, the daughter of the Earth, is deeply connected to nature. Her time in the forest, her calm amidst the trees of Ashoka *Vatika*, and her eventual return to Mother Earth symbolize her purity and closeness to nature. I, too, feel a deep connection to the natural world. The flowers I weave into garlands for Lord Vishnu represent my pure love, just as the trees and flowers in the Ashoka *Vatika* bore witness to Sita's unshaken purity and devotion.

Both of us find comfort in the simplicity and purity of nature. Just as Sita remained untouched in her devotion despite the worldly trials around her, I seek to maintain my purity of heart, offering only the purest love to my Lord through the flowers I gather and the songs I sing.

Sita's return to Lord Rama after the great battle of Lanka is a beautiful moment of reunion - one that signifies the triumph of love, faith, and devotion. I, too, await the day when Lord Ranganatha will come to me and take me as His bride. Just as Sita was carried away in Rama's chariot back to Ayodhya, I dream of the day when Lord Vishnu will take me to His eternal abode in *Vaikuntha*.

Sita's devotion to Lord Rama and my devotion to Lord Vishnu express the same eternal love. We both represent the power of a devoted soul to remain steadfast in love, regardless of the challenges we face. In Sita, I see the strength to endure, and in my own heart, I feel the same unwavering dedication to the Lord.

Her story, though different in its circumstances, mirrors my own in its essence: love, longing, patience, and faith. Both of us are symbols of surrender and devotion, showing the world that true love for the divine transcends time, space, and earthly trials.

Like Sita, I long for union with my beloved Lord, Ranganatha. Rama's journey reminds me that devotion requires patience, endurance, and faith, and I pray for the strength to walk this path with the same dedication He showed.

Balarama (The Strong Brother of Krishna)

Balarama, the elder brother of Krishna, is an *avatar* of Vishnu known for His immense physical strength and deep sense of duty. Often depicted with a plough, Balarama is also associated with agriculture and the fertility of the Earth. He played a crucial role in supporting Krishna during His adventures and was a fierce protector of dharma. His plough, symbolic of both sustenance and destruction, represents His ability to nurture and to uphold justice when needed.

Balarama's story reminds me of the importance of balance - between nurturing life and standing firm in righteousness. His strength, both physical and moral, inspires me to cultivate the same in my own life. As the protector of Krishna and the Earth, Balarama teaches me that love for the Lord can take many forms, whether through nurturing or protecting what is sacred. I pray to have the same strength and steadfastness in my devotion as Balarama showed in His loyalty to Krishna and His protection of dharma.

Krishna (Cowherd and Prince)

Lord Krishna, the eighth incarnation of Vishnu, is perhaps the most beloved of all *avatars*. His life is a divine play (*leela*) filled with joy, love, and wisdom. As a child in Vrindavan, He enchanted the *gopis* with His flute and performed miraculous feats, while as a prince in Dwarka, He provided guidance and leadership to His people. His teachings in the **Bhagavad Gita**, imparted to Arjuna on the battlefield of Kurukshetra, are a timeless guide to living a life of dharma, devotion, and surrender.

The story of Krishna fills my heart with joy and devotion. His playful *leela* in Vrindavan, His mischievous nature, and his deep love for Radha and the *gopis* speak to my own longing for the divine. Krishna teaches me that love for the Lord can be expressed in the simplest moments of joy and play. His wisdom in the **Bhagavatam** also guides me, reminding me that life's challenges are opportunities to surrender to the Lord's will and trust in His plan. In Krishna's life, I see a reflection of the eternal dance of love between the soul and the divine.

Kalki (The Warrior of the future *Avatar*)

Kalki, Lord Vishnu's final *avatar*, is prophesied to appear at the end of the Kali Yuga, the current age of darkness and corruption. Riding a white horse and wielding a sword of justice, Kalki will descend to destroy the forces of evil and restore righteousness to the world. His arrival marks the end of the current cycle and the beginning of a new age of peace and virtue.

The story of Kalki, though set in the future, fills me with hope and anticipation. Even though the world may seem lost in darkness, the Lord will return to restore balance and dharma. Kalki's arrival reminds me that His justice is inevitable no matter how far the world may stray from righteousness. I trust that Lord Vishnu will always intervene when the time is right, and this knowledge gives me the strength to remain steadfast in my devotion. I pray to be ready for His return, my heart filled with faith and love, knowing He will come to save us all and restore divine order.

Each of Lord Vishnu's *avatars* holds a special place in my heart, teaching me different aspects of devotion, dharma, and divine love. From the humble Matsya to the fierce Narasimha, from the playful Krishna to the future warrior

Kalki, I am constantly reminded of His infinite compassion, wisdom, and power. These stories fill me with devotion and faith, knowing that God, in every form, is always with me, guiding me toward His divine embrace.

In every form, I am yours

As I sat, listening to the stories of your *Avatars* from my father, my realization of the love I feel for you grew stronger with each word. With every tale of your divine incarnations - your form as Rama, as Krishna, as Narasimha - I felt an unexplainable connection. It was as if I knew you from before, as if our love has transcended lifetimes, moving through the cycles of existence. In each *Avatar*, I could feel your presence, your essence, and your proximity to me. With every story, I felt my heart beat in rhythm with yours, as if I was not merely hearing the tales, but reliving them with you, knowing that our souls have been entwined across time. Each incarnation of yours speaks to a different facet of my devotion, drawing me closer to the truth that I am forever yours, and you are mine.

As a girl in love, every part of my being belongs to Him. My love isn't just about devotion; it's a deep, all-encompassing desire to offer myself to Him in every way - physically, emotionally, and spiritually. I don't live merely as a devotee; my entire existence is an offering to Him, and with each breath, I yearn for the day when I will be completely one with my beloved Lord.

My physical beauty, though admired by others, holds no value for me unless it's for Him. I adorn myself daily, not to impress the world, but to present myself as a garland to Him, just as I weave flowers around His divine image. When I look into the mirror, it's not out of vanity but out of a longing to see how I might appear to Him, hoping to offer the finest version of myself. Each flower I place in my hair, each bracelet around my wrist, is not mere decoration - it is a silent prayer: *"Take me, O Perumal! I am Yours, fully and completely."* I want my physical form to reflect the love I carry inside, a symbol of my youth, beauty, and vitality offered solely to Him.

Just as Sita waited patiently in her unwavering love for you during your Rama *avatar*, I too am ready to wait, no matter how long it takes. Sita's patience, her silent strength as she waited for you, her beloved, to come for her, is the patience I carry within me. My love is steady and enduring, as hers was - no obstacle, no hardship can dull the flame of my devotion. I wait, not with longing for worldly pleasure, but with the certainty that my soul is already united with you, and our reunion is inevitable. *Just as Sita waited in faith, so will I, forever.*

I am consumed by an intense and overwhelming love for Vishnu. There is no separation between us - He is in every thought, every breath. When I sing, it's not just a melody; it's my soul calling out to Him. And when I cry, my tears don't come from sorrow but from the sheer intensity of my love. *I want to dance with You the way Radha danced with You in your Krishna avatar* - a dance not of feet, but of souls. The way Radha danced, her entire being surrendered to you, her love pouring out through every step, every turn, was a reflection of the divine connection between the two of you. Radha's love was boundless, and through her dance, she offered her soul to you. I too wish to offer myself through the dance of my emotions, my movements guided by the rhythm of my heart, which beats for you alone.

Sometimes, I am overcome by emotions so powerful that I am left speechless, in soulful tears, feeling a deep ache and a profound joy at the same time. These emotions are not mine alone - they are vessels for my devotion, carrying me like a river seeking the endless ocean of Your love. *My tears flow like the tears of Bhoomadevi in your Varaha avatar, each drop a prayer, a plea, an offering.* And like the mountains and rivers that surrendered to Your divine strength in that form, I too surrender all of myself to You, letting Your love shape me, guide me.

I desire nothing less than a complete union with Vishnu. For me, devotion is not just about rituals or prayers - it's about dissolving all boundaries between myself and the divine. My deepest longing is to merge with You, to lose myself in Your divine presence and become one with You in the truest, most complete sense. Every verse I compose, and every song I sing, brings me a step closer to this union.

I see myself as a bride, not waiting for a mortal groom, but for You. *I wish to embrace You, like how the ocean embraced You in your Kurma avatar.* The way the ocean held you, steadying the divine churning of the cosmos, I too wish to hold You in my soul, to become the stillness that steadies Your divine presence in this world. *I want you to guide me, like how You guided humanity as the enlightened Parashurama.* My love for You goes beyond the human experience of devotion - it is pure, boundless, and impossible to express fully. You are my home, my safe place, just as you were for Prahlad. *I am ready to endure anything for You, just as the great Bhakta Prahlad endured so much for his unwavering faith in You.* I would give anything to feel the embrace of Your divine hands, as Prahlad must have when You emerged in Your Narasimha form to protect him.

Songs of my Soul

There are moments when the weight of my emotions is too much for me to carry alone. I feel them pressing against my chest, longing to be spoken, but when I try, no sound escapes. My heart holds a love so vast that words feel too small to contain it. I look around, wanting to share what stirs inside me, but I find that no one can truly understand the depths I feel. It's not that I don't wish to speak, but how do you explain a love that touches the very core of your being?

So, I have taken to writing. When my voice fails, my pen becomes my voice, speaking all that my heart cannot. In the quiet, when the world is still, I let my soul pour into words. Each word, each rhyme, carries a fragment of what I wish I could say aloud. My poems have become my whispers to the universe, my secret prayers to Narayana. I weave my feelings into simple lines, but within them lies the essence of everything I am and the love I feel for Him. It is here, in the simplicity of words, that I find the courage to release what I have held so tightly within.

When I write, it's as though I'm speaking to Him directly. Every poem I write is a letter to my beloved, a piece of my soul offered in devotion. Each line is a whispered prayer, each rhyme a silent confession to Narayana. In those quiet moments, with my words as my only companions, I am able to pour my soul out without fear, without hesitation. My words are my way of reaching for Him, of telling Him all that my heart holds, even when my voice cannot. Through my poems, I say what my heart has longed to speak in His presence. The words may be simple, but within them, I find the freedom to express the love, the longing, and the devotion that courses through me like a river.

I write of the moonlit nights when I feel His presence most strongly, of the moments when my heart aches to be near Him, and of the joy I find in the simplest acts of devotion. In the quiet of my writing, I feel His gaze upon me, as though He reads every word with a knowing smile. It is in these quiet, solitary moments that I feel closest to Him, as if my soul is reaching out to His, bridging the distance between us.

The more I write, the more I realize that this is how I was meant to speak to Him. My poems are not just words; they are my offering, my heart laid bare before Him. In these verses, I surrender everything I am - my fears, my desires, my dreams. Writing has become my sanctuary, the space where I can be truly vulnerable. With each word, I weave a tapestry of love and longing, hoping that somehow, through these humble lines, He hears me.

I have come to understand that it is not always in the grand gestures or spoken words that love is felt most deeply. Sometimes, the most profound love is found in the quiet spaces, in the words we dare not speak aloud. My poems have become the voice of my soul, telling the story of a love that transcends lifetimes, a devotion that stretches beyond the limits of words. Through the rhythm of rhyme, I touch the eternal, knowing that my love for Him lives on the page, just as it lives within me.

Each rhyme is a prayer, each verse a confession of my devotion. Writing has become my sanctuary, a place where I can be vulnerable, where I can be truly myself. It is through these lines that I feel closest to Him, as though the very act of writing draws me into His embrace, calm and soothing.

Vishnu in the Clouds

I woke before dawn that morning, as I always do, to offer my prayers to Lord Vishnu. But something felt different. As I lit the lamps at His altar, a soft breeze stirred the *Tulsi* leaves outside, making them whisper His name, and a faint rumble echoed in the distance. I stepped out of my small house, barefoot on the cool earth, and looked up at the sky. Dark clouds had gathered, heavy and full, covering the horizon like a thick blanket.

There was something stirring in the air, a feeling of anticipation, as if the whole world was holding its breath. I stood still for a moment, listening to the silence that comes before a storm. Then, without warning, the wind picked up. It swept through the garden, rustling the leaves, twisting the flowers, and sending shivers down my spine. I pulled my shawl closer, but the wind didn't feel cold. It felt alive, like it was carrying something divine, something beyond this world.

I closed my eyes and let the wind wrap around me, feeling it lift my hair and tug at my clothes. It was as if the wind itself was trying to speak to me, to remind me of something. Suddenly, a loud crack of thunder split the sky. I opened my eyes, startled, and saw the clouds swirling above me, dark and heavy with rain. Lightning flashed, lighting up the sky for a brief moment, and in that instant, I could see Him - Vishnu, in the clouds, watching over me.

I could feel Him. The storm wasn't just a storm; it was His presence. The wind, the rain, the thunder - it was all Him. I lifted my face to the sky, my heart racing with love and anticipation. The clouds rumbled again, louder this time, and then the heavens opened up. Rain began to pour down in torrents, drenching the earth and everything around me. But I didn't move. I couldn't. I felt rooted to the ground, as if Vishnu Himself had placed His hand upon me, holding me in place.

This is You, O Ranganatha. You are in the wind, in the rain, in the thunder. I can feel You everywhere.

The rain soaked through my clothes, dripping from my hair, but I felt no discomfort. In fact, I felt more alive than I ever had. The rain wasn't just water - it was like a blessing from Him, washing over me, cleansing my soul, reminding me of His love. Each drop felt like a touch from Him, soft yet powerful, and I stood there, arms open wide, welcoming it. *When the rain touches me, it feels as if You are touching my soul,* I whispered softly. My clothes clung to me, my hair dripping, but in that moment, I felt nothing but love, a love so vast it enveloped me completely. The rain was Him. It was His way of reaching me, of holding me close. The sky flashed with lightning, illuminating the world in a brief, blinding light, and in that moment, I could almost see Him. My Lord Vishnu, standing there in the rain with me, His eyes filled with the same love I felt in my heart. I could see His hand reaching out, inviting me to join Him, to come closer.

You are here, O Narayana. I feel You in the rain, I see You in the storm.

Then came the wind again, stronger this time, swirling around me, pulling at the trees, whipping the flowers into the air. The sky was alive with the sound of the storm, thunder cracking, wind howling, rain pounding the earth. But I wasn't afraid. I knew this was His way of showing me that He was near. The storm was His love, fierce and unyielding, just as my devotion to Him was. It was as if the elements were dancing with me, a divine rhythm created just for us.

In every gust of wind, I feel Your breath. In every clap of thunder, I hear Your voice.

As the rain continued to pour, I spun in circles, my hands lifted toward the sky, my heart overflowing with joy. I felt as though I was dancing with the storm, with Him. Each step I took felt light, as though the earth beneath me had disappeared, and I was floating in His presence. I twirled faster and faster, losing myself in the movement, in the rain, in the love I felt surrounding me.

For a moment, the thunder silenced, and everything around me stilled. I stood there, panting, soaked to the skin, the wind still swirling gently around me. I looked up at the sky, and through a break in the clouds, I saw a single ray of sunlight streaming down, cutting through the dark. It touched the ground right in front of me, lighting up the wet earth, and I smiled. I knew it was His light, a reminder that even in the storm, He was always there.

Then, as quickly as it had begun, the storm began to subside. The rain slowed to a drizzle, the wind softened, and the clouds began to drift away, leaving the sky clear and bright. The air was fresh, clean, filled with the scent of wet earth and flowers, and I stood there, soaked and breathless, feeling as if I had just touched the divine.

You are the storm and the calm after. You are the wind and the stillness that follows.

I walked slowly back toward the altar, my heart full of His presence. As I knelt before Vishnu's image, the water still dripping from my clothes, I felt a deep sense of peace. The storm had passed, but its energy, its love, remained with me. I knew that He had sent the rain, the wind, the thunder to remind me that I was never alone. He was always with me, in every drop of rain, in every gust of wind, in every beat of my heart.

No storm is too fierce when it is filled with Your love, O Lord Vishnu.

That night, as I lay on my mat, listening to the soft drizzle of the remaining rain, I smiled to myself. The storm was not just nature's force. It was Vishnu's way of telling me that He was always near, always watching, always loving. And as I drifted off to sleep, I felt the lingering warmth of His presence, knowing that no matter what storms may come, I was His, and He was mine, forever intertwined like the clouds and the wind.

No storm, no rain, no distance will ever keep me from You. You are in every drop, and I am Yours, now and forever.

The Worn Garland

Sitting in the *Tulsi Vanam*, I carefully weave a garland for my beloved Narayana. The yellow and red roses blend beautifully with the sacred *Tulsi* leaves, creating something truly enchanting. As I finish, I wear the garland as usual and glance into the steel plate I always carry - a humble mirror for moments like these. Placing the garland around my neck, I can't help but admire its beauty. How radiant my Narayana would look adorned with this garland!

Suddenly, a voice pierces the air

Kothai! Kothai! What have you done? You've committed a grave sin by wearing the garland meant for Lord Narayana! Why would you desecrate such a sacred offering?

The hurt in his voice crushed me. I had never meant to disrespect the Lord; my actions had come from a place of love. But in my father's eyes, I had broken a sacred rule.

I apologized to my father, assuring him I wouldn't repeat the mistake of wearing the garland before offering it to Narayana. My words were meant to comfort him, but deep inside, my heart doesn't believe I committed any sin, as he said. Yet, I let it be. My father is older, and I respect his wisdom. I will obey, even if my heart feels differently. All I can control is my devotion, so I pour all my love into my prayers for my beloved Narayana.

Lately, though, I've noticed a change in Him. He no longer smiles or teases me like before. When I dress Him in His *dhoti* or adorn Him with necklaces and crowns, He wears them without complaint. There was a time when He would playfully refuse, insisting on choosing His garments or demanding I place the flute in His hand a certain way. But now... He's quiet. He wears whatever I give Him without a word, eats without spilling, and seems distant. It's as if He's lost the playful joy we used to share. I can't understand why. What have I done, my Lord? I miss His laughter, His teasing, His vibrant presence. I am left in confusion, longing for the days when He would make mischief to see me smile.

Nothing is changing. The air is still, and Narayana remains as distant as before. His smile does not return, his eyes remain fixed, and the playful joy that once filled the room is nowhere to be seen. I stand there, waiting for something - for any sign that He has accepted this offering, that He has felt my love. But there is only silence. My heart aches, knowing this is not what He wanted. He is waiting for something more, something deeper.

One evening, as the temple grows quiet and the last of the visitors leave, I return. The moon is high in the sky, casting a soft glow over the temple grounds. I make my way to His sanctum once more, but this time, my hands are empty. I stand before him with no garland or flowers - just my heart, bare and full of questions. I kneel before him, my forehead resting against the cool stone floor.

Narayana, tell me, how can I reconcile this? How can I honor my father's wisdom while staying true to the love you have shown me? You are the Lord of my heart, and yet, I cannot disobey the one who raised me in your devotion. How do I follow both paths without causing pain?

I have been doing this for many days now, but he is silent. My heart breaks, and I feel pain. *I cannot be without you O Ranganatha. I cannot bear this silence*, I tell him, asking him to show me the way.

Last night, after so many days of silence, He came to me in my dream and revealed what had been troubling Him: He no longer finds joy in the garlands because I no longer wear them first. He longs to feel the garland that has already touched me, that carries my love and devotion before it is placed upon Him. My heart swells with this revelation, for it confirms what I always felt - my love was never a sin. It was the purest emotion I have known and felt.

But what of my father's beliefs? He truly feels that I have been committing a transgression by wearing the garland before offering it to Narayana. In his eyes, I was defiling a sacred gift. Yet, in my heart, it was always an act of love, a way to offer my Lord the best of me.

Now I find myself torn between what my father considers a sin and what my heart knows is love. Narayana, guide me. Please show me the path. Should I continue obeying my father's wishes, or should I follow the truth revealed by Him? I stand at the crossroads of duty and devotion, yearning for Your light to show me the way.

Acceptance of the Worn Garland

The morning sun bathes the temple in golden light, but my heart is clouded with doubt. Yesterday's revelation weighs heavily on me. I walk quietly to the *Tulsi Vanam*, my feet tracing the familiar path, yet everything feels different. My fingers tremble as I gather the sacred *Tulsi* leaves, and the fragrance of roses fills the air, but my mind is elsewhere. I am torn between my duty to my father and the truth that Narayana revealed in my dream.

How can I stand before Him with a garland that doesn't carry the fullness of my love? How can I offer something that lacks my essence when he has shown me what he truly desires? Yet, how can I disobey my father, who has guided me in devotion for as long as I can remember? I feel the weight of both worlds pressing down on me, my heart heavy with the dilemma of choosing between the two.

I finish weaving the garland, its delicate petals intertwined with the sacred *Tulsi* leaves. Today, I don't look in the mirror. Instead, I gaze at the garland in my hands, wondering if Narayana will feel the love I poured into it, even though I did not wear it first. Will He miss the touch of my skin, the imprint of my devotion, like He revealed in my dream? The thought tugs at my heart.

I hand over the garland to my father, and in silence, we make our way to the temple. I walk slowly to the inner sanctum, my steps hesitant. We approach the sanctum sanctorum, and the familiar sight of Him fills me with both comfort and longing. He sits there, adorned in silk and jewels. His eyes were serene but distant. Today, as I approach, I find myself whispering, *Perumaale, My Lord, what should I do? Should I follow my father's words or the truth of the love you revealed to me?*

As if sensing my hesitation, everything seems to fall silent around me. The temple is quiet, and the soft rays of the early sun stream through the carved windows, casting warm patterns on the stone floor. For a moment, I hesitate. I can feel the pull in my heart, the desire to honor His request, to give Him the garland as He wishes - to offer Him the love that has touched me first. But my father's words echo in my ears, telling me to follow the sacred traditions.

My father places the garland around Narayana's neck.

As he does so, something strange happens. The lamp that always burns steadily beside His image begins to flicker. At first, I thought it was just a draft, but as my father reached to adjust the flame, it went out entirely. Confused, he relit it, only to see it flicker and die again. The lamp keeps going out as if something unseen is blowing it out each time. My father looks at the lamp with furrowed brows and then at me, a hint of surprise in his eyes. We are still surprised when the knot of the garland opens, and it falls off Narayana's neck.

Kothai, this has never happened before, he says softly, his voice filled with concern.

Narayana's smile tells me that I must find balance, that the true offering is not just the garland - it is my heart, the purity of my love, the sincerity of my devotion.

I lower my gaze, and at that moment, the weight of my dream comes crashing back to me - the dream in which Narayana told me He longed for the garland to touch me first. It wasn't just a dream; it was His will. He had shown me what He truly desired, and now, He is showing us both.

I take a deep breath and turn to my father, my voice quiet but steady. Father, there is something I need to tell you. *Last night, Narayana came to me in my dream. He told me that He no longer finds joy in the garlands I offer unless I wear them first. He wishes for the garland to touch me before it touches Him.*

My father stares at me, silent for a long moment. His eyes search mine, and I can see the hesitation, the weight of tradition and belief pressing down on him. But I also see something else - understanding, a quiet acceptance. He is a man of deep devotion, and I know that, despite his initial shock, he trusts in Narayana's will.

My father looks at me, and I can see the hesitation, the weight of tradition and belief pressing down on him. But I also see something else - understanding, a quiet acceptance. He is a man of deep devotion, and I know that, despite his initial shock, he trusts in Narayana's will.

For a moment, he is silent, and I worry he will not understand. But then he sighs a deep, thoughtful sound.

Kothai, he says, his voice soft but steady, *you have always been different. Your devotion goes beyond what most can comprehend. If Narayana himself desires the garland to touch you first, then who am I to stand in the way? If the Lord desires this, who are we to deny Him? I may not fully understand it, but I trust your love for Him.*

He takes the garland, ties the knot, places the garland in my hands, and then, in a voice, that is soft but resolute, says, *Kothai, wear the garland.*

With trembling hands, I take the garland and place it around my neck. The moment it touches my skin, I feel the familiar warmth of love and devotion enveloping me. It feels right as if this is how it was always meant to be. My father watches me closely, and without another word, he takes the garland from me and places it gently around Narayana's neck.

He lit the lamp again. The lamp, flickering just moments ago, now springs to life. The flame grows stronger and brighter, illuminating every corner of the temple with a radiant light that seems almost otherworldly. My father and I exchanged a glance of wonder, our hearts pounding with the sudden energy in the air. It was as if the very air had shifted, as if the temple itself was filled with Narayana's joy. The light is no ordinary flame - it glows with a radiance that seems almost divine, as though Narayana Himself is pleased.

The lamp's flame dances high, and in the flickering light, something miraculous happens.

Within the bright, flickering flame, we both see it - a vision of Lord Vishnu. His divine form appears in the light, shimmering with grace and beauty. His eyes, filled with love and kindness, look upon us as if to confirm His joy in the offering. My father gasps beside me, his voice caught in his throat. I stand frozen, overwhelmed by the sight of Narayana's radiant image. His presence fills the temple, and it feels as though the very air is vibrating with divine energy.

My father, usually so composed, is overwhelmed with emotion. His eyes are wide, and his voice trembles as he speaks. *Kothai… this is a miracle. Lord Vishnu has revealed Himself to us.*

He bows deeply, tears in his eyes. I, too, feel tears welling up from the overwhelming love I feel from Narayana, the Lord who accepts me as I am.

The flame continues to burn brightly as if blessing us both with its radiant glow. The vision of Narayana lingers for a few moments longer before gently fading. But the peace and joy in the temple remain, filling every corner and every heart.

In that moment, I know. Narayana's love is as vast as the sky, and he accepts the offering of my heart just as it is. My father's heart, too, is at peace, for he now understands that devotion comes in many forms and that true love for the Lord transcends tradition. Together, we stand before Narayana, the lamp still burning brightly, and I know that this moment will stay with us forever.

My father, usually composed, is overcome with emotion. *Kothai, Lord Vishnu has accepted your love*, he says, his voice trembling with reverence. He addresses me as *Sudikodutha Sudarkodi* (the one who offered the garland to Perumal after adorning it). He places his hand on my head to bless me and show his ineffable happiness.

I bow deeply before Narayana, my heart swelling with gratitude. The burden that once weighed on my soul is lifted, and I feel lighter than I have in days. I understand now that it was never about tradition or ritual - it was always about love, about offering what was pure and true from the depths of my heart. Narayana doesn't desire the garland untouched. He desires it to carry the essence of my devotion for Him.

In the evening, I sit in the *Tulsi Vanam* again, weaving another garland. This time, my heart does not hesitate; instead, it is filled with a beautiful lightness. When I finish, I place the garland around my neck, feeling the familiar warmth of love course through me. I don't look into the steel plate this time - there is no need. I feel the garland on me and smile softly, knowing that the garland, touched by my devotion, is perfect for Him.

The world around me mirrors the peace within me. When the garland is around Narayana's neck, the air hums with joy. His eyes sparkle, His lips curve into the playful smile I have missed so dearly, and the temple feels alive with His presence once again. The flame dances brightly, as if celebrating the bond between us.

Thank you, Narayana, I whisper, filled with love and gratitude. Soulful tears fill my eyes, and I feel peace. At that moment, I know that everything is as it should be. His love is eternal, and

He has accepted me, my garland, and my devotion.

His smile shines brighter than ever, a silent promise that our bond is as strong as ever.

The Dance of Devotion

It was a warm afternoon in Shrivilliputhur, the air thick with the fragrance of jasmine and the distant din of temple bells. I had spent the morning in prayer, offering garlands of flowers to my Lord Vishnu, but my heart felt restless.

I stepped out of the temple into the courtyard, my feet bare against the cool stone floor. The sun was dipping low, casting golden light across the temple walls, and a soft breeze stirred the air. It was quiet, serene, but inside me, there was a rhythm - an energy that I couldn't contain any longer.

I walked to the center of the courtyard, and without thinking, I began to dance. It was not a conscious decision; it was as if my body had been waiting for this moment. My feet moved in time with the beat of my heart, and my arms stretched toward the sky, reaching for Him. I could feel His presence, as though He was watching me, waiting for me to express my feelings.

O Ranganatha, I cannot speak what my heart feels, so let me dance for You. Let every step, every gesture be a prayer, an offering to You.

I spun, my skirt flaring out around me, and I felt lighter, as if the weight of the world had lifted from my shoulders. My hands moved through the air, painting invisible patterns, each one a message of devotion. My feet struck the ground with a rhythm that echoed in the empty courtyard, a rhythm that wasn't just mine, but His as well. I was dancing not for myself, but for Him.

In this dance, I become Yours completely, losing myself in the love I feel for You.

With every movement, I felt His presence closer, like a warm breeze enveloping me. I twirled faster, the earth beneath me disappearing as if I was no longer bound by the ground. I was floating, dancing in His presence, each step taking me closer to Him, each spin making me feel more united with my Lord.

The world around me faded - there was no temple, no town, no sky - just me and Him, dancing together in a realm beyond this one. I imagined His divine form beside me, His soft smile watching my every move, His eyes filled with love and grace. I twirled toward Him, reaching out as if I could touch Him.

I felt the rhythm of the universe in my dance, as though each step I took aligned with the cosmic flow of creation. My feet moved faster, my arms stretched wider, and I felt the energy of my love for Him grow stronger, filling every inch of my being. I was no longer a girl in a temple; I was a soul dancing with the divine.

The sun had set, but I didn't notice the sky darken or the stars appear. I was lost in my devotion, my body moving with a grace I had never known before. I spun again, faster, my hair whipping around me like a halo, my heart beating in perfect time with the rhythm of the universe, with the rhythm of Him.

And then, in a moment of stillness, I stopped. I stood in the center of the courtyard, my breath heavy, my chest rising and falling, but my soul calm, at peace. I could feel Him. Vishnu was here, not as a distant deity in the temple, but as a presence inside me, around me, filling the air I breathed.

I knelt on the ground, my knees pressing into the cool stone, my heart still racing from the dance. The silence around me was profound, and in that silence, I could hear His voice - not in words, but in the way the night wrapped itself around me, in the way the stars blinked into existence overhead. I felt Him in every part of me, as if He had been dancing with me all along.

The night was now bathed in moonlight, and the air was cool against my skin. I sat in quiet reverence, feeling the connection between us stronger than ever. I realized that my dance had not been mine alone. It had been a dance of two souls, a dance of union, a dance of love. In that moment, I felt closer to Him than I ever had before.

With every step, every spin, I am closer to You. In my dance, I have found You, and in You, I have found myself.

A Heart full of Love

When one's heart is full of love, the world itself transforms. The light within me spills over, and suddenly, everything around me becomes a reflection of that love. It is as though my soul, brimming with affection for the Divine, can now see His presence in all beings, in every corner of creation.

Love begets love. When the heart is truly immersed in it, love does not remain a singular emotion held tightly within, but rather, it radiates outward, seeking to connect, to uplift, to heal. In love, the boundaries between 'I' and 'You' blur, and the Divine weaves itself into the very fabric of life.

I have seen this with my own heart, which beats only for my Narayana. In the depth of my devotion, something wondrous has unfolded - my love for Him has begun to mirror itself in every living soul I encounter. It is as if by loving Him so deeply, I have learned to see His spark in every being. The farmer working the fields, the child playing in the street, the birds that sing at dawn - all of them now appear to me as reflections of His essence.

In love, the ordinary becomes extraordinary. A simple glance at the sky feels like a glimpse into eternity. The soft rustle of the wind through the trees becomes the whisper of the Divine. Even the trials and tribulations that life presents no longer feel burdensome, for they, too, are part of this cosmic dance of love. It is love that allows me to see beyond the surface, to feel the divine pulse in every creature, to recognize the beauty that lies within each soul.

When my heart is full of love, I cannot help but feel the Divine's presence in everyone I meet. His essence, though unseen by the physical eye, is felt in the smallest gestures - a kind smile, a thoughtful word, or even in the silence shared between two souls. This love is not bound by conditions or expectations; it simply flows, abundant and free, seeking no return. It fills the heart and overflows, touching everything in its path.

In loving deeply, we unlock a vision that transcends the limitations of the mind. We begin to see not with our eyes, but with our hearts. The flaws and imperfections of others fade into insignificance when viewed through the lens of love. What remains is the truth - that we are all connected by this same divine thread of existence.

In this way, love becomes a prayer, an offering, and a source of divine connection. It is love that binds me to Him, and it is through love that I see Him in all creation. When the heart is full of love, the world is no longer merely a place to live; it becomes a sacred space where the Divine resides in all things.

The Vrindavan Within

Alisha

I have always longed to visit Vrindavan, the sacred land where Krishna once walked, where His divine pastimes unfolded. The thought of being in the same place where He had danced with the *Gopis*, played His flute by the Yamuna, and filled the air with His enchanting presence consumed my heart. I wish to walk through the narrow lanes, my lips chanting His name, my heart beating in rhythm with the memories of His divine play. To be in Vrindavan, to feel the very ground that Krishna had touched, seems like the ultimate fulfillment of my yearning.

Last night, as I drifted into sleep with thoughts of Vrindavan in my heart, I had a dream so vivid, so powerful, that it felt more real than the reality itself. In the dream, I was in Vrindavan, by the banks of the Yamuna, bathed in the golden light of the setting sun. The river shimmered with a soft glow, and the breeze carried the sweet fragrance of jasmine and *Tulsi*. There, amidst the serene beauty of nature, I saw Him - Krishna, my beloved, sitting by the river, His flute resting in His hands, His eyes filled with the mischievous charm that only He possessed.

Without a word, I found herself drawn to Him, my heart overflowing with joy. Krishna smiled at me, a smile that made the world around me melt away. I began to sing for Him, my voice soft and melodious, carrying the songs of my soul that I had always wanted to sing. As I sang, He began to play His flute, and the melody that flowed from it was unlike anything I had ever heard - sweet, soothing, and filled with a love that seemed to encompass the entire universe.

I found myself dancing in the dream, my feet moving effortlessly, as though guided by His music. I danced with Him, my heart filled with bliss, every movement a prayer, every turn a celebration of our divine love. It was as if the world around us had vanished, and all that remained was the sacred bond between my soul and Krishna. The dance was not just a physical movement - it was the union of our spirits, a merging of my love with His divine presence.

As the music softened, I found myself sitting beside Krishna, resting my head gently on His shoulder. The cool breeze from the Yamuna rustled through the trees, and Krishna continued to play His flute, the sound resonating in my very soul. It was a moment of profound peace, a stillness that made everything else fade into insignificance. I felt safe, content, as though I had finally found my place in the universe - beside Him, with Him, lost in the music of our love.

When I got up in the morning, the dream lingered in my heart, so real that it blurred the lines between dream and reality. For a moment, I couldn't tell if I had truly experienced those moments by the Yamuna or if it had all been an illusion of her mind. The peace, the joy, the completeness I had felt in the dream were so overwhelming that it seemed impossible they were not real. I sat in silence, trying to grasp the beauty of what I had just experienced, but the more I thought, the more I realized something profound.

It wasn't Vrindavan that my heart truly longed for. It wasn't the physical place where Krishna had walked - it was the union with Him that I craved. The dream had shown me that it wasn't about being in Vrindavan, it was about being with Him. My soul yearned for the connection, the oneness with my beloved, more than any earthly destination. The realization struck me deeply - what I truly desire is not a pilgrimage to Vrindavan, but a sacred union with my beloved.

Krishna's presence in the dream has made me realize that my ultimate goal, my only true desire, is to be one with Him.

Even if it takes my entire lifetime, even if I have to wait through the endless cycles of time, I am content to live in this longing. I am ready to wait, to embrace the beauty of this waiting, because I know that ultimately, my soul will find its way to Him. Every moment of this waiting only deepens my love, and I cherish even the yearning as a gift. My heart, my soul, and my life are all devoted to that single desire - to be one with Him.

In Surrender, we Give; in Love, we Belong

When I move through the world, when I walk the streets of Shrivilliputhur, it is as though I am in two places at once. My body moves in this world, but my heart, my soul - they are always with You. I hear the chatter of people, I see the bustle of life around me, but none of it reaches me. It is like watching a distant dream, a world that exists beyond my true reality. My true reality is You, O Ranganatha. My true existence is in Your presence.

My love is like the dawn, soft yet powerful, like the wind, invisible but ever-present, like the rain, pouring itself completely, holding nothing back. My love is a river, flowing with purpose toward Him, the ocean waiting to receive me. It is the stars in the sky, tiny but steadfast, always burning. It is the moon, reflecting His light, sometimes full, sometimes just a sliver, but always there, waiting to shine.

I see my love mirrored in nature - constant, boundless, eternal. My heart reaches for Him, just as the earth turns toward the sun, as rivers flow to the ocean, as the wind whispers its devotion through the trees.

One evening, I watched a Chakor bird chase the moon, unwavering in its devotion, even though it could never reach it. In the bird, I saw myself - endlessly longing for Narayana, always chasing, knowing that true love doesn't need to possess. It is the act of loving, the devotion itself, that gives life meaning.

Like the Chakor, I will forever reach for Him, my eyes always on Him, my heart always wanting His presence. Even in this unfulfilled desire, I find Him, for it is in the longing that I feel closest to Him.

His love is not something I can step away from. It is not a momentary thought or a fleeting feeling. It is a constant presence, as vital to me as the air I breathe or the food I eat. There are moments when I forget where I end and He begins, as though our souls are already entwined, inseparable. My mind cannot think of anything but Him, my heart cannot beat without the rhythm of His name.

I am consumed, and I welcome it. To be consumed by His love is the greatest blessing I could ever receive. I feel no fear, no hesitation in giving myself completely to Him, for I know that my purpose, my very existence, is to be His. The world may call me Andal, but I know the truth - I am already a part of Him. My soul, my love, my devotion - they have all been swallowed up in the ocean of His presence, and I am lost in Him.

Sometimes I wonder if He feels it too, this all-encompassing love that has overtaken every part of me. Does He know how completely I have surrendered myself to Him? Does He feel the way my heart aches with longing for Him, the way my soul yearns for His touch, His presence, every moment of every day? I believe His does. I believe that just as I am consumed by my love for Him, He too holds me within His divine embrace.

In my heart, I believe that if Perumal ceased to be, my entire world would crumble. The sky, the earth, the sun, the stars - all of creation would collapse into nothingness. He is the force that holds everything together for me. He is the breath in my lungs, the beat of my heart, the light in my eyes. Without Him, all of my existence would lose its meaning. I do not simply worship Him. I live through Him, and He lives through me. There is no separation, no distance between Him and Me. My love is so pure, so absolute, that I can not imagine a world where He does not reign in my heart.

For me, there is no existence outside of Him, no meaning without Him. My entire being is wrapped up in His essence, and I know that if He is by my side, my world will forever be filled with light. But if He ever leaves me, if His presence ever fades from my life, the world itself would lose its color, its vibrancy. Flowers would wither, the rivers would dry, and the stars would fall from the sky. For me, He is not just the center of my world. He is The world. Everything else is a mere shadow compared to the brilliance of His love. If he is there, only then will I exist. If he is not there, the universe will collapse, and I will vanish into the void, for my world is not the earth or the sky - it is Him, and Him alone.

Overwhelmed by these thoughts during my meditation, I light a lamp and try to convey my deep feelings -

O Narayana, my Lord, You are not just the object of my love. You are my love itself, the fire that burns within me, the force that moves me, the light that guides me.

I am no longer just Andal. I am a soul consumed by your divine love, by the longing to be one with You, by the desire to merge so completely into You that there is no separation left between us. Every breath I take, every step I walk, is for You. I exist only for You, and in that existence, I find all the meaning, all the purpose I could ever need.

There is nothing left of me, O Narayana. There is only You, only this love that has swallowed me whole. And I am content, for in this love, I have found my home. In this love, I am complete, consumed by the divine fire of Your presence, and I never wish to be free from it. I am Yours - now, always, and forever. Consumed by Your love, I live only in You, for You, with You.

Am I Worthy of His Love?

He who is the Lord of Lords, the ruler of the cosmos, the one who holds the universe within His hands - how could someone like me, a simple girl, ever expect His love? I think of this often as I sit beneath the *Tulsi Vanam.* He is beyond everything. He is the creator, the protector, the eternal one, and I am just a simple girl whose heart overflows with longing for Him. How could I ever be worthy of His love?

O Narayana, You are infinite. You are the Lord of all that exists. And yet here I am, with nothing but my love to offer You. Why would You look upon me? Why would You ever accept me as I desire?

These thoughts swirl in my mind day and night, though my heart refuses to let go of the hope that He sees me and feels the intensity of my devotion. I know what others may say - that I am a mere mortal, that my love is a drop in the ocean of His greatness. But my heart cannot help but dream. Yes, I am a simple girl, but my love is not simple. My love for Him is boundless, pure, and fierce. It consumes me completely, as though my soul was born only to love Him. I may not be worthy in the ways the world understands, but my heart believes that true love has its way of being worthy.

Why would He love me back? I ask myself again and again. The thought of Him surrounded by celestial beings, adored by the gods and goddesses, His divine form radiating a light that transcends human comprehension, makes my heart tremble. What could I, a simple girl, ever offer Him that would make Him look at me with the same love that I feel for Him?

And yet, my heart whispers a different truth. Love doesn't follow the rules of this world. It doesn't care for worthiness in the way we think of it. Love is not measured by titles or status, by greatness or power. Love exists in the quiet spaces between hearts, in the silent moments where nothing else matters but the connection between two souls.

Could it be, I wonder, *that He sees my love for what it truly is? Not a love that seeks reward or recognition, but a pure love that asks for nothing but to be close to Him?* I think of the times when I have prayed to Him in the silence of the early mornings when the world is asleep, and it's just Him and me. In those moments, I feel His presence so profoundly, as though He is listening to the very beat of my heart. Does He not feel that love? Does He not see how completely I have given myself to Him?

Why would He love me? I ask again, and this time, the answer comes not from my mind but from my soul: *Because love does not ask for reasons. It simply is.*

Perhaps He sees in me what I see in Him. A soul that longs for union, that craves a connection beyond this world. Perhaps He sees my love, my devotion, my surrender, and knows that I have nothing to offer but myself, and yet that is the greatest gift I could give. I am not a goddess. I am not a celestial being. I am just a simple girl with flowers in my hands and prayers on my lips. But my love is true, and in that truth, I believe He finds something worthy.

O Narayana, do You know? I ask quietly as I light a lamp for him. *Do You know that I love You not because I seek Your greatness, but because I see You as my beloved, my everything? You are the Lord of Lords, yes. But You are also the Lord of my heart.*

I imagine Him smiling softly, his eyes full of understanding. He does not need grandeur or perfection. He wants what is real and genuine. And my love, in all its simplicity, is real. It is pure. It is everything I have to give. Perhaps that is why, despite my doubts, I feel that He loves me - not because I am great, but because my love makes me worthy.

I think of the stories of Radha and Krishna, of how Radha, a simple girl from Vrindavan, captured the heart of Krishna, the divine *avatar* of Vishnu. Radha's love was pure, untainted by the world's expectations. It was the love of the soul, not the body, and that is why Krishna loved her so deeply. He did not care that she was not a queen or a goddess. He saw the truth of her heart, and that was enough.

Could it be the same for me? I ask myself. *Could my love be enough for Him in its raw, unfiltered form? Could He love me not despite my simplicity but because of it?*

I believe that He could. I believe that He does.

O Narayana, You are the Lord of the universe, but to me, You are my beloved. I do not ask for You to make me worthy. I ask only that You see the truth of my love, the depth of my devotion. And if You see that, perhaps You will love me as I love You - completely, without reason, without condition. I say as I bow down in front of him to do my *Namaskaarams.*

With that thought, I smile softly to myself. For in my heart, I know that no matter what, I am His, and He is mine. And that is all the reason I need.

A Father's Tender Heart

My father has always been my guide, my teacher, and, in many ways, he has given me the purest form of motherly love. Though I was found beneath the *Tulsi* plants and not born from him, he has never made me feel anything less than cherished, as if the Lord Himself placed me into his arms to be cared for with a love so deep, it goes beyond words.

I've always felt like my father's devotion to Lord Vishnu spills over into his love for me, as though by caring for me, he is, in some way, fulfilling his service to the Lord. But his love is also so tender, so gentle, it often feels as though he carries the heart of a mother within him. He has never once treated me as an obligation or a duty, but as his own, raising me with a nurturing spirit that sees beyond the earthly bonds of father and daughter. In his eyes, I see the reflection of both a protector and a nurturer, as though he carries both the masculine and feminine aspects of love within him.

There are times when I recall the small moments where his motherly care came through. I remember one night, as a little girl, I had fallen ill. My body burned with fever, and I felt so weak I could barely move. Though my father rarely rested himself, spending long hours in prayer and caring for the temple, he sat beside me through the night, his hand gently on my forehead, his touch so soothing it felt as though the fever itself was afraid to linger. I remember waking up in the middle of the night to find him softly chanting verses from the scriptures, his voice a balm to my soul. His words were not just prayers to Vishnu; they were a mother's lullaby, easing my pain, watching over me with such care.

He prepared the simple remedies with the same devotion he showed in tending to the *Tulsi* plants. I could see the concern in his eyes, yet he never wavered, his touch light, his presence calming. He would hold a small bowl of herbal medicine to my lips, coaxing me to drink with the same tenderness I imagine a mother would, whispering softly, *Drink this, Kothai, it will help you heal. Vishnu is watching over you.* It wasn't just his words, but the way he said them, that made me feel wrapped in the warmth of his love.

There was another time when I had spent hours playing in the garden, my hands busy gathering flowers to make garlands for the Lord. The sun had been harsh that day, and by the time I returned home, my skin had burned and my body ached from exhaustion. My father, seeing the redness on my cheeks, didn't scold me for overworking myself; instead, he gently bathed my arms in cool water, wiping my face with a cloth dipped in sandalwood paste to soothe the burns. He braided my hair, his fingers as delicate as any mother's, and as I lay there, I felt a kind of love that was so complete, it reminded me of the stories I'd heard of how mothers care for their children.

At times, my father would even tell me stories to lull me to sleep, much like a mother might. He would sit beside me in the evenings, the lamps lit softly around the house, and tell me about the divine pastimes of Lord Vishnu. His voice, calm and soothing, would carry me into a world where

Vishnu walked among us, where His love was everywhere, much like the love I felt from my father. One of my favorite stories was when he told me about Lord Krishna in Vrindavan, how Yashoda, His mother, would chase Him as He ran through the fields, laughing and playing. I would drift off to sleep imagining that I, too, was cradled in such motherly love, but instead of Yashoda, it was my father's love that protected me.

Even when I felt confused or overwhelmed by the intensity of my devotion to Vishnu, my father never dismissed my emotions. There was a time when I found myself crying late at night, overcome by the longing to be close to Vishnu, to offer myself to Him completely. My father found me sitting in the *Tulsi Vanam*, tears streaming down my face. Instead of brushing away my feelings or offering hollow words of comfort, he sat beside me, gently wiping the tears from my cheeks. He didn't say much, but his presence, his soft hand resting on my shoulder, was enough. It was the kind of comfort that I imagine a mother would give - a wordless understanding, a silent reassurance that I was not alone.

And then there was the small, quiet gestures that made me feel wrapped in his motherly care. Every morning, he would carefully prepare the offerings to Vishnu, but not before checking that I had eaten. Sometimes, he would place a small bowl of fruits or milk by my side, urging me to take care of my body, just as a mother would. He would insist I rest after long days of prayer or temple duties, always reminding me, *Kothai, even Vishnu wants you to be healthy and strong. You must take care of yourself to serve Him.*

In my father's love, I have always felt a sense of balance - a love that is both strong and protective, yet nurturing and tender. Though he is devoted to the Lord in every way, he has never neglected me. He has cared for me with a love so complete that I have never known the absence of a mother's affection. Through his actions, I have learned that true love is both divine and human, masculine and feminine, all-encompassing in its ability to nurture the soul.

I often think that Vishnu, in His infinite wisdom, gave me to my father not only to receive spiritual guidance but to be enveloped in a love that is as nurturing as it is divine. My father is my source of unending support and love, nurturing me in every possible way so that I may grow into the devotee I am meant to be. And just as he found me in the sacred *Tulsi Vanam*, he has continued to nurture the divine spark within me, guiding me toward the ultimate love that binds us all to Lord Vishnu.

A Prayer Answered In The *Tulsi* Garden

Though he rarely openly discussed it, my father had a deep and unfulfilled longing to have a child. He was always so devoted to Perumal and focused on serving the Lord that he didn't often share his desires. But sometimes, in quieter moments, he would reveal glimpses of that deep yearning, especially when he spoke of the divine stories of Krishna's birth.

As a child, I would sit beside him in the evenings while he gathered the villagers around, telling them stories about Krishna, his divine *leelas*, and the sacrifices made by those who loved Him. One story he often told was that of Devaki, Krishna's birth mother. He spoke of her pain, her anguish after giving birth to Krishna, only to have him taken away from her to protect Him from the wicked King Kamsa. My father's voice would soften as he described how to keep Krishna safe, Vasudeva carried Him across the Yamuna, through the stormy night, to Yashoda, who raised Krishna as her own.

There was always something in my father's voice, a tenderness, a deep understanding when he spoke of Devaki's sorrow. He would often pause, his eyes growing distant, as if he were feeling that very pain himself. It wasn't just the story of Devaki's sacrifice that moved him - it was the experience of a parent's love, of the longing to hold a child close and keep them safe. Though he often brushed it aside with a smile, I could feel the weight of his unspoken desire to be a father, to experience that deep connection.

He would talk about how Devaki knew that Krishna was meant for something greater despite the heartbreak of parting with her newborn son. She sacrificed her joy as a mother for her child's safety, trusting in the divine plan. But my father always emphasized how difficult that must have been to have her baby taken from her arms, not knowing when, or if, she would see him again. I often sensed that he was reflecting on the yearning that he had as he spoke of these stories, as if through Devaki's loss.

One night, after he had finished telling the story to the villagers, I asked him why he spoke so often of Devaki's pain. He smiled at me, but there was a sadness in his eyes, a depth of emotion I didn't fully understand then. *You see, Kothai,* he said softly, *the love of a parent is a sacred thing. Even Devaki, knowing that her son was the Lord Himself, felt the pain of separation. She longed to hold Him, to raise Him, but she had to give Him up for His safety. A parent's love is like that - it's full of sacrifice and longing, even when you know your child belongs to the world or to something greater.*

It was only later, as I grew older, that I realized how much my father had longed to have a child of his own. For years, he had devoted his life to Lord Vishnu, offering everything he had to the service of the divine. But in his heart, there was a quiet longing - to hold a child in his arms, to share his wisdom, his love, and his devotion with someone who would continue his legacy of faith. The story of Devaki's sacrifice must have resonated deeply with him, for he, too, knew the pain of longing for a child he thought he might never have.

When I was found in the *Tulsi Vanam*, I can only imagine how that longing in his heart was fulfilled. The way he tells the story, it's as if Vishnu Himself answered his prayers by placing me, a baby, right in the sacred garden he tended with such care. He often says that when he saw me lying there, nestled among the *Tulsi* leaves, he felt the same awe and joy that Devaki must have felt when she first laid eyes on Krishna. In his heart, I wasn't just a child - I was a divine blessing, an answer to the prayers he had whispered over the years in the quiet hours when he was alone with his thoughts.

Looking back now, I understand my father's deep love for me and the way he raised me with such tenderness and devotion, always ensuring that I knew I was loved beyond measure. He never once let me feel like I was anything less than a miracle in his life. I was his daughter, but more than that, I was the fulfillment of a longing he had carried for so long - a longing to love, to nurture, to share his life and devotion with a child.

Though he rarely spoke of it directly, I know that every time he told the villagers about Devaki's pain and sacrifice, a part of him also spoke of his own journey, his own love, and his own fulfillment. I was his daughter, but I was also the child he had always prayed for, and in caring for me, I believe he felt the completion of that sacred longing he had carried in his heart for so many years.

He would always finish the story by telling how my coming had made him feel complete. As he spoke of Devaki's longing for Krishna and the fulfillment she must have felt when she was finally reunited with her son, he would glance at me with a quiet smile. He would tell the villagers that, just as Devaki's heart was made whole by Krishna's return, so was his own heart made whole when he found me in the *Tulsi Vanam*. He would say, *The Lord answered my prayers in His way by blessing me with a daughter who filled the space in my heart that I didn't even know was there. Kothai, like the garlands she makes, has woven her love into my life, and in her presence, I have found the joy and completeness I had longed for.*

Hearing him say this always filled me with a deep sense of belonging. I knew that my presence was not just a miracle for him but a fulfilment of something far bigger than either of us could fully comprehend. His stories were never just about the gods - they were also about us, about the love we shared, and about how, in finding me, he had found the child he had always prayed for.

The Coming of Andal

It was a Friday, and the moon was high in the sky, casting its bright, silvery light across the small town of Srivilliputhur. The moon seemed to shine with an unusual brilliance that night, turning everything it touched into a soft, glowing silver. My father describes how the light gently blanketed the *Tulsi Vanam,* our sacred garden, bathing the plants in an otherworldly glow. The air was cool, carrying the fragrance of jasmine, mingling with the earthy scent of *Tulsi* leaves. It was the kind of night where everything felt still, where even the breeze seemed to whisper something sacred, and the world held its breath in quiet anticipation.

As he always did, my father spent his evening in the garden, caring for the *Tulsi* plants, offering his love to Vishnu through his gentle touch and soft hymns. But that night, he says, something was different in the air. It was a quiet he couldn't place - a heavy stillness with something waiting to be revealed. He hadn't prayed for anything specific that evening, but his heart was always packed with devotion.

He tells me that when he woke up and went to the *Tulsi Vanam* before dawn, the garden shone brightly in the beautiful moonlight. It felt divine, and as he started tending to the plants, something caught his eye. There, nestled beneath the *Tulsi* leaves, bathed in the moonlight, was a small, still figure - a baby. He found me lying there, wrapped in the moon's glow, my eyes wide open, looking up at the stars as though I already understood them. He says I wasn't crying, nor did I make a sound, just peacefully resting among the sacred plants, as if the earth had cradled me in its arms.

For a moment, my father says, he was frozen. How could a baby be here, in the heart of the *Tulsi Vanam*, under the moon, on a night filled with serenity? But deep inside, he knew. He knew this was no ordinary moment and no ordinary child. His hands trembled as he lifted me from the ground, bringing me close to his chest. He says he felt an overwhelming sense of completeness, as if, in that moment, his heart found something it had been waiting for without knowing it.

He named me *Kothai* right then, meaning "garland." Just as he wove garlands for Vishnu every day, he felt that I, too, was a divine garland placed into his life by the hand of Vishnu Himself. I became not just a child but a living gift sent by the divine on that moonlit night.

The following day, the news spread through the village. People came to the *Tulsi Vanam,* their faces full of awe and wonder. They saw me resting in my father's arms, and many of them bowed their heads in reverence, convinced that my appearance was a sign, a blessing from Lord Vishnu. My father says some of them spoke of the night before, how even they had felt the air change, how the moon seemed to shine more brightly as if preparing for something divine.

Even now, my father tells me, every time on Aadi Pooram night, he feels a sense of calm and divine presence, as though the universe remembers the night I was found. He never forgets how the world seemed to stand still that night and how the moon and stars bore witness to my arrival. Every time he tells me the story, I can hear the gratitude in his voice, the awe that still lingers in his heart. It was a night that changed everything, when, beneath the light of the moon, my father's prayers were answered in the most miraculous way.

The Search for A Groom

Lately, my father has been talking more and more about finding a groom for me. He does it with such care, gently mentioning new families, new names, each one with hope in his voice. I know he wants the best for me, just like any father would. His dreams are simple - he wants to see me married, settled, and happy.

All around me, my friends are getting married. Every time I see them, they speak of their weddings, their grooms, their new lives with such excitement. I watch them, trying to smile, but inside, I feel distant. Their joy, their anticipation - it's not mine. My heart doesn't leap at the thought of a wedding; instead, it aches with a longing I can't explain to anyone, not even my father. While they dream of husbands and homes, my heart is already bound to someone beyond this world.

I love my father deeply, and I know he has always dreamed of seeing me as a bride. He imagines the day I will be dressed in a saree, surrounded by music and joy, starting a new life with a husband by my side. It's what every father wishes for his daughter, and I can see it in his eyes every time he talks about my future. But he doesn't know the truth I've been carrying in my heart, the secret that weighs me down every time he speaks of marriage.

The truth is, I can't marry anyone. My heart belongs only to Narayana, my divine beloved. Since I first felt His presence, I've known that my love could never be given to anyone else. I have surrendered everything to Him - my heart, my soul, my everything. How could I ever be a bride to anyone in this world when I already feel married to Him? But how do I tell my father this? How do I shatter the dreams he's held for me all these years?

I sit with him each evening as he talks about potential grooms, his voice filled with excitement. Each new proposal feels like a knot tightening in my chest. I want to make him happy, to be the daughter he's always envisioned, but I can't live a lie. I can't go through with something that would tear me away from the love I've already given. Still, I don't know how to find the words to explain this to him. I can't bear the thought of breaking his heart.

One evening, as the sky turns from gold to deep blue, I know I can't hold it in any longer. My father sits by the window, lost in thought, the room quiet except for the soft rustling of leaves outside. I walk over to him, my heart pounding in my chest, and sit beside him. The weight of what I'm about to say makes my hands tremble.

Appa, I begin softly, my voice barely steady. He turns to look at me, his eyes full of love and concern. He can sense something is different.

I know you've been searching for a groom for me, I say, taking a deep breath. *And I know you have dreams for my wedding, just like every father does. But... I can't marry anyone.*

He looks at me, confused, but says nothing, waiting for me to continue.

My heart... it already belongs to someone else, I whisper, the words feeling heavy but also like a release.

Who? he asks, his voice gentle, though I can see the confusion deepening.

I take a deep breath. *Lord Vishnu, Appa. I've given myself to Him, completely. I can't imagine being with anyone else. My heart is His. I don't want to marry any man.*

I take a deep breath, trying to steady myself, but before I can speak, my father interrupts, his voice tender but firm. *I understand your devotion, Kothai,* he says, the concern in his eyes clear. *But love is different. This is devotion to God, but marriage... marriage is for this world, for living a life with a partner by your side. How can you marry God Himself? I will find a good man for you, someone kind, someone who will cherish you. I will make sure you live a happy married life with him, just like your friends. You deserve that, my child.*

Hearing him say this breaks my heart a little, but I know I cannot bend to his wishes. *No, Appa,* I reply, my voice soft yet unwavering, *I know it's hard to understand, but my heart doesn't belong here in this world. I don't want a worldly marriage. My soul... it is already bound to Narayana. When I place the red kumkum on my forehead, I feel as though my soul is married to Him. Every thought, every breath I take, it's for Him. I cannot give my heart to anyone else because it already belongs to Him. It's not just devotion, Appa - it's love. A love that has filled every part of me. I see no future with any man, only with my beloved. He is my everything, my eternal companion.*

There's a long silence. My heart pounds in the stillness, every second feeling like an eternity. I can't bring myself to look at him, fearing the disappointment, the pain I might see in his eyes.

Finally, I hear him take a deep breath. *You've always had a special connection, haven't you?* he says, his voice softer than I expected.

I look up, surprised by the calmness in his voice. There's no anger, no frustration, just understanding.

Kothai, my dear, if your heart belongs to Him, then I won't stand in your way. I bless you, my daughter, and may Lord Vishnu bring you the happiness you seek. He says after a moment, his eyes filled with love and soulful tears. *I only want you to be happy.*

Tears well up in my eyes as I reach for his hand, overwhelmed by the relief and gratitude I feel. I had feared this moment for so long, worried about breaking his heart, but he has given me the greatest gift - his acceptance. He sees the path I have chosen, and in his love, he has given me the freedom to walk it. I reach for his hand, my heart full of gratitude and love for the father who, despite his dreams for me, has chosen to honor mine.

As I sit there, holding his hand, I know I've finally spoken my truth. And in that truth, I've found peace.

The Gypsy's Prediction

The day began like any other. I was in the garden, surrounded by the vibrant scent of flowers, sitting under the shade of the *Tulsi* plants. The golden morning light filtered through the leaves, dappling the earth with soft patterns. I sat quietly, weaving a garland for my beloved Narayana, just as I had done every morning for as long as I could remember. My hands moved with familiarity, picking the freshest of flowers, their soft petals mingling with the sacred *Tulsi* leaves.

As I threaded the flowers together, my heart was full of Him. Narayana. Every thought, every breath, and every action of mine was dedicated to Him, and I longed for nothing more than to be with Him, to be His bride. Each petal I touched was my love transformed into a physical offering, each fragrant blossom an unspoken prayer for Him to notice me, to accept me. In my mind's eye, I could already see Lord Ranganatha, resting gracefully at Srirangam, His eyes kind, His smile playful, waiting for me.

Yet there was always the distance, so far beyond my reach, between this earthly realm, where I existed, and the divine world, where He resided. Deep in my heart, I knew I was destined for more than this world could offer. I was destined to be His.

As I sat absorbed in these thoughts, a figure appeared at the edge of our garden, breaking the peaceful stillness. I looked up, surprised to see a stranger approaching. He was unlike anyone I had ever seen. His clothes were worn and rough, his skin weathered by the sun, and he carried the air of a wandering gypsy. There was a wildness in his eyes, but behind that, a mischievous glimmer I couldn't quite understand. I stared at him, confused but curious. Who was this man, and why had he come to our humble home?

He approached with ease, as if he belonged, and my father, Periyalvar, who had been nearby, quickly came forward to greet him. My father, ever kind and hospitable, invited him in, though there was a hint of wariness in his gaze. It was rare for strangers to visit, especially someone who looked like this - a gypsy or perhaps a wandering hunter, with a quiver slung over his shoulder and beads adorning his neck.

The man smiled, his eyes twinkling, and I couldn't help but feel there was something unusual about him. He seemed out of place, yet somehow, there was a sense of familiarity in the way he moved, as though he were more than just a wandering traveler.

The gypsy accepted my father's hospitality and sat down in our home. His presence was casual yet commanding. My father offered him water and a simple meal, as is our custom. The man thanked him, speaking with an easy charm that seemed to fill the room. He told stories of far-off places, of forests where the birds sang songs no human had ever heard, and of rivers that sparkled like jewels under the moonlight. His words were captivating, and yet, something in me remained alert, wondering why he had truly come.

Then, his gaze turned to me, and his smile grew even wider. He seemed to study me for a moment, his eyes lingering, before he asked a question that pierced straight through me.

So, young one, he said, his voice light but his words carrying weight, *have you found a husband yet? Have you decided who will share your life?*

His question was so sudden and direct that I felt my heart skip a beat. For a moment, I was stunned. He had no right to ask me such a thing. Yet his eyes held mine, and something deeper was behind the playfulness. I felt a strange pull to answer, as if something far more significant than a simple conversation was happening.

Without hesitation, I answered, my voice steady but filled with conviction. *I will marry no one but Lord Narayana. My heart belongs to Him, and no one else could ever take that place.*

The man chuckled softly, but it wasn't mocking - it was as if he were amused by my response, as though he already knew what I would say. He leaned forward slightly as if sharing a secret.

Are you sure? he asked. *You've never seen Lord Vishnu in person. You've only heard stories and sung His praises. Perhaps if you met someone who truly loved you - someone standing right in front of you - you might change your mind.*

For a brief moment, doubt tried to creep into my heart. His words were carefully chosen, meant to make me reconsider. But I felt my resolve grow even stronger. I knew what I wanted, what I had always wanted - Lord Vishnu was not just a distant figure in my prayers. He was the one I was destined to marry and to whom my heart belonged.

I looked at the stranger, my voice firm, *No. My love for Narayana goes beyond what my eyes can see. I feel His presence in my very soul. He is with me, even when He is not visible to the eye. There is no one else for me. No earthly man could ever compare to Him.*

The man's playful smile softened, and the room seemed to grow still for a moment. The air felt heavier, as though something sacred was about to unfold. I could feel the energy around me shift, and then, something incredible happened.

The man before me, this mysterious gypsy, began to change. Slowly, the roughness of his clothes faded away, and a brilliant light began to shine from him. His simple garments transformed into the finest silks, shimmering like the sun. Jewels appeared on his chest, and a golden crown adorned his head. His wild, rugged appearance dissolved, revealing a divine form that made my heart stop.

Before me stood not a gypsy, but Lord Kallazhagar Himself, the Lord of Thirumaaliruncholai, one of the many forms of Lord Vishnu. His eyes, which had once sparkled with mischief, now glowed with a deeper affection - a love that radiated from Him, filling the entire room with a divine presence.

I experienced a moment of breathlessness. The Lord, my beloved Narayana, had come to me, not as I had imagined Him, but in a form that tested the very core of my devotion. He had come in disguise to see if I could still recognize Him and if my love for Him would falter when He appeared as a mere man.

Tears welled in my eyes as I realized the truth. The Lord had come to me, not as a distant deity but as a playful and loving companion, wanting to test if my love was pure and my devotion could stand firm against doubt.

Lord Kallazhagar smiled softly at me, and at that moment, I felt as if my entire soul had been lifted. He spoke to me in a tender and powerful voice: *Andal, your love is true, unwavering, and eternal. You have proven that no matter the form I take, your heart remains steadfast. You have passed the test, my dear Andal. You are indeed destined to be Mine.*

I fell to my knees, overcome with joy and reverence. My Lord, the one for whom I had waited, had come to me. Though He had tested me in disguise, my heart recognized Him. I had proven my love to Him, and He had accepted it.

The Lord looked upon me with such love, and I could feel His divine grace surrounding me. He told me that my longing, prayers, and devotion had reached Him and that soon, I would be united with Lord Ranganatha at Srirangam. My heart soared with joy at His words.

He had come not only to test me but to bless me. He reassured me that my dream of marrying the Lord was not just a fantasy but a divine reality. The Lord of the universe Himself had acknowledged my devotion, and my deepest desire to be His bride was soon to be fulfilled.

Before He departed, Lord Kallazhagar left me with a profound truth. He told me that love, true love, goes beyond appearances and beyond earthly rituals. He reminded me that the Lord does not always come to us in the ways we expect, but if our love is pure and unwavering, we will recognize Him, no matter the form He takes.

With that, the Lord disappeared, leaving me with a sense of divine peace and fulfillment. The air seemed to hum with His presence, and I knew this moment would stay with me forever.

After the Lord's departure, I sat with my father, both of us overwhelmed by what had just happened. I could see the awe in his eyes, and together, we knelt in prayer, thanking Lord Vishnu for His grace and for revealing Himself to us.

From that day on, I felt a new sense of peace and certainty in my heart. I knew that my love for Narayana had been accepted and that soon, I would be united with Him. The Lord had tested me, and I had remained steadfast. Now, I waited for the day when I would be taken to Srirangam, where I would finally be His bride.

Thus, the Lord Kallazhagar came to me in disguise, not to confuse me, but to see if my love was true. And now I know, without a doubt, that no matter what form He takes, I will always recognize Him. For my love for Narayana transcends appearances and reaches the depths of my soul. Soon, I will be with Him, just as He promised.

In His Love, I Find My Home

From the moment I could understand the world around me, I knew I had but one desire, one purpose, one truth that consumed my entire being. It wasn't wealth, fame, or the fleeting pleasures of this earthly life. It was Him - my Lord Vishnu. My heart, soul, and everything I am have always been dedicated to Him alone. There was never a doubt in my mind, never a moment where I wavered. My one desire, my only goal, was to be united with Him, to merge with His divine presence so that there would never again be separation.

In every heartbeat, there is only His name; in every breath, there is only His love. If one were to ask me, "Why do you love Him?" I would have no answer, for there is no reason. How can there be a reason when love is this pure, this complete? *Love does not ask why; it simply knows.*

In Him, I find my beginning, my end, my forever. When our hearts beat as one, my love will find its eternal home. It's not just a hope; it is my certainty. I know that this longing, this love I feel for Him, will be answered one day. I don't see my life as a series of events but as one continuous movement toward Him. My entire being is focused on this single truth: I belong to Him, and it fills me with purpose every single day.

One afternoon, I sat by the temple steps after offering my prayers. The sun was setting, casting a warm golden light across the sky. I closed my eyes, allowing the serenity of the moment to wash over me. As I sat there, I felt a soft hand rest on my shoulder. Startled, I opened my eyes and saw no one. But I could still feel the presence, gentle yet firm, as if Perumal Himself had placed His hand on me, telling me, *I am with you always.* I know people talk of worldly goals - of ambition, of desires, of achieving greatness. But to me, there is no greater goal than to be united with my beloved Vishnu. My devotion is unwavering, and my heart is single-minded in its purpose. There is no distraction, no temptation strong enough to pull me away from this path. My father tells me that anything can be achieved if there is total clarity and complete focus. And for me, there is nothing clearer than this: I am His. Every iota of my being is dedicated to this sacred union, and I know that one day, I will feel His presence not just in my prayers, not just in my heart, but in every part of my soul. I will become one with Him, never to be apart again. This is my desire, my love, my life - and I will see it fulfilled.

In His love, I find my purpose; in His union, I will find my eternity.

Patience is the purest form of Love

The evening sky was tinged with soft hues of orange as I make my way to the temple, my heart filled with anticipation. Tonight, I will dance in devotion, offering my heart through each graceful movement. But my thoughts, as always, are with him - my beloved, the one I have loved with a depth no one can truly understand. He has spoken to me in my dreams, promising that our union would come, but I have to wait. I have to be patient.

Patience is the purest form of love, I remind myself, *because it trusts in a future already written by destiny.*

I will wait for eternity if I have to. My devotion for Narayana is not bound by time or circumstance. I trust him completely, my heart is filled with his love. And tonight, as the temple is celebrating a festival in his honor, I will dance for him, knowing that even if our union has not yet come, my devotion will reach him.

As I arrive at the temple, my eyes widened at the sight of the ongoing construction. The grand temple halls, where I had imagined my dance unfolding, are hidden behind scaffolding. The sanctum where I had longed to offer my devotion is inaccessible. Instead, a temporary stage has been set up outside, under the open sky.

A pang of disappointment touched my heart, but I quickly pushed it aside. This place, this moment, is still sacred. Whether inside the temple or out in the open, my love for Narayana would shine just as brightly. The temporary stage is enough - it will be the platform for my devotion, my dance of love.

I step onto the stage, and as the music begins, my body becomes an instrument of my heart, moving with grace and purpose. The world around me seemed to melt away, and all that is left was me is my love for him. My body became an instrument of my devotion, each step, each gesture flowing from the depths of my soul. I dance for him, for my beloved, lost in the rhythm of love and faith.

As the music swirled around me, something deeper stirred within me - a realization that grew with every movement. The stars above seem to flicker with an ethereal glow, as if they are watching me, twinkling in appreciation. The moon, full and bright, cast its gentle light upon me, serene and peaceful, as though it too feels my devotion. The breeze whispers through the trees, carrying my love on its currents.

And in that moment, I feel it - the vastness of the universe. Not just around me, but within me. My dance was not confined to the small stage beneath my feet; it is a part of something much larger, something cosmic. In loving him, I have found the universe within me. The stars, the moon, the earth beneath me - they were all a part of me, just as my love for Narayana is a part of the universe itself.

Tears well in my eyes, spilling over as my emotions become too much to hold back. The waiting, the longing, the devotion I had carried in my heart - it all came rushing out in a torrent of love. But with that love came a realization that struck me like a wave.

I am not simply waiting for Him. There is more to my journey than just our union. The universe within me, the vast love I feel - it is meant to be shared. My purpose isn't just to love Narayana in secret, waiting quietly for him to come. I am meant to spread his name, to sing his praises, to tell the world of his glory. That is why he has asked me to wait. Not because I am not ready, but because my love has to reach beyond myself, beyond my own heart, to the hearts of others.

My tears flow freely now, but they are no longer tears of craving or longing. They are tears of understanding, of a love so great it can no longer be contained within me. Love isn't about waiting for the perfect moment - it's about living every moment with the fullness of your heart. I will no longer wait passively for our union, but will live, fully and openly, sharing my devotion with the world. I will sing Narayana's glories with every breath, dance his stories with every step, and let the whole world know the depth of my love.

As the realization took hold of me, my dance changed. My movements become more powerful, more filled with purpose, as though the universe itself flowed through me. I am not just dancing for myself, or even for Narayana. If love asks me to wait, I will wait. But I will not wait silently. I will live, sing, and dance in his name. I am dancing for the world, for the souls who need to know the beauty of his name, the magnificence of his love.

True love doesn't count the days of waiting; it lives in the certainty of union.

My heart swells with joy, my soul at peace with the waiting. I know now that this time, this life, is not just for yearning, but for living, living to spread Narayana's name, to share my love for him with all who will listen. I will use this time to pour my devotion into every corner of the world, telling his stories, singing his praises, filling every heart with the love I have felt so deeply.

My heart swells with joy, my soul alight with the truth I have always known. The highest form of love is devotion, and devotion is not idle - it is active, it is alive. In every breath, I feel him. In every moment of waiting, I love him more deeply. For the more I wait, the more I love. The more I love, the more I become a part of him.

And when the time comes, when Narayana finally calls me to him, I will be ready, not just as the woman who loved him, but as the one who had shared his love with the world.

With the stars twinkling above, the moon smiling down, and the universe embracing me, I dance, not in waiting, but in living. And in every step, my love for Narayana spreads like a fire, lighting the world with its glow.

The Divine Dreams

For days now, my nights have been filled with dreams so vivid, they feel more real than waking life. In these dreams, my beloved Vishnu comes to me, His presence so close, so tangible, that I can feel the warmth of His love surrounding me. Each time I close my eyes, He is there, and it is as though the distance between us is finally disappearing.

In these dreams, I see myself dressed as a bride, adorned with the finest flowers, garlands of jasmine and lotus woven into my hair, my body draped in the most exquisite silk, shimmering in the soft light. My heart feels light, yet full, as I stand beside Lord Ranganatha, the reclining form of Vishnu at Srirangam. His divine form rests peacefully, yet I can feel His energy, His love radiating toward me. I know He is watching me, though His eyes are closed, His presence filling every part of my soul.

As I stand there, I hear His voice - deep, soothing, and filled with love. He speaks to me, telling me what my heart has longed to hear for so many years. *You have fulfilled your destiny, Kothai,* He says, calling me by the name that feels like a melody only He can sing. *Your love has reached Me, across all realms, and now the time has come. I am coming to take you as My bride.*

His words fill me with a peace so profound, I can barely contain it. My heart, which has known nothing but longing, now knows only joy. In His voice, I hear the promise I've waited for, the confirmation that everything I have lived for, prayed for, and offered has been received by Him. Every tear, every verse, every moment of devotion has led me to this - our union.

These dreams are not like others. They do not fade away upon waking. Even now, as I open my eyes and look around at the familiar world, I can still feel His presence lingering, as if He has just left the room but remains in the air I breathe. The scent of the flowers from my dream still clings to me, and my heart is filled with bliss. I know, with every fiber of my being, that this is not an ordinary dream. This is a divine promise.

I have lost count of His dreams now, and each time, it feels even more real. I see myself standing closer to Him, my hand reaching out toward His. I can feel the weight of His promise settling in my heart, growing stronger with each passing day. I know that my beloved Vishnu is near, that our long-awaited union is not just a hope but an imminent reality.

The peace that fills me now is unlike anything I have ever felt. All the longing, all the yearning that once consumed me has transformed into pure joy, into the sweet anticipation of knowing that I will soon be with Him, not just in spirit, but in the truest, most complete union. My soul is ready. I am ready.

I am no longer just waiting; I am living in the certainty that Vishnu is coming for me. Every breath I take, every beat of my heart, carries me closer to Him. And when the time comes, I will stand before Him as His bride, just as I have seen in my dreams. I will lay down everything at His feet, and in that moment, our love will become eternal, just as I have always known it was meant to be.

The Full Moon's Promise of Reunion

The *Purnima*, or full moon night, has always captivated my soul in ways I can hardly explain. Under the full moon, the soul remembers what the mind cannot fathom. There's an inexplicable pull on me, as if the moon's soft, glowing light awakens memories buried deep within me. Every time I stand beneath the full-lit sky, a profound sense of peace washes over me - a feeling not just of comfort but also of belonging. It's as though I've lived this moment countless times, under this very same moon, in another life, another realm.

The full moon, with its silvery glow bathing everything in an ethereal light, feels like a doorway to another world, a world where I am no longer bound by the limitations of time or space. Beneath this celestial brightness, I feel as though I've been transported to a place that's deeply familiar yet beyond my reach. The full moon holds the memory of every moment I've ever shared with Him, a silent witness to our love across lifetimes. There's a pull that's both gentle and undeniable, as if the moon itself whispers to me of a time long ago when my soul was entwined with my beloved Narayana's in a dance as timeless as the stars.

In these moments, I can almost feel the presence of my beloved Narayana beside me. I close my eyes, and the world around me fades. I see myself twirling in the moonlight, dancing with Him, as He stands there with His flute, playing a melody that speaks directly to my heart. The tune is soft and enchanting, wrapping us in a world of our own. I dance not just for the joy of it but for Him - for the smile that lights up His face when He sees me lost in the music of His love.

I can feel His gaze upon me, a look so tender and filled with love that it fills my heart to overflowing. His eyes hold a depth that reflects the universe itself, and in that gaze, I find everything I've ever sought - peace, love, and belonging. In His gaze, I see a universe more vast than the stars, more eternal than time. Each movement of my dance is for Him alone, an offering of my heart, my soul, my very being. And as He watches, I can see the corners of His lips curve into a smile that lights up the night more brilliantly than the full moon above us.

As we pause in our celestial dance, I present Him with a bowl of His favorite *payasam*, the sweet dish I've prepared with love and devotion. I can almost smell the sweet aroma of the *payasam* that I've prepared with such care, knowing it brings Him joy. In the smallest act of devotion, I find the greatest expression of my love. I offer it to Him with love, and I see Him smile, the simple act of sharing this moment with Him filling me with the deepest contentment. I know He treasures every bite as much as I treasure preparing it for Him.

We sit together on the *oonjal* (swing), gently swaying under the full moon's gaze. The moonlight filters through the leaves above us, casting soft patterns of light and shadow over His face, making Him look even more divine.

In the rhythm of the swing, I feel the pulse of our love, timeless and eternal. I lean my head on His shoulder, feeling the warmth of His presence as if this is where I was always meant to be. In this moment, I am content beyond words, as if everything I've ever yearned for has come to rest right here, in the quiet intimacy of our shared silence.

In this sacred silence, no words are needed - just the comfort of being together, as if time ceases to exist when we are with one another. In the sacred stillness of the night, His presence speaks louder than any words ever could.

Under the full moon, I am reminded of the countless times we've been here before, in the past, living out these same sacred moments of love.It's as though these moments have lived inside me forever, not as dreams or fantasies, but as memories of a time when my soul danced in divine union with Him. Love like this knows no bounds, no time, no beginning, no end - it simply is, just as the moon that forever lights the night sky. The full moon brings them back to life, reminding me of a love that transcends lifetimes, a connection that feels as eternal as the moonlight itself.

The full moon is more than just a celestial event; it's a reminder of the eternal bond that exists between my soul and His. Each time the *Purnima* comes, it brings with it the promise of reunion, the feeling that no matter where I am or how far I may stray, under this radiant sky, I will always find my way back to Him. Every full moon is a reminder: no matter how far we may wander, we will always find our way back to the one who holds our heart. And so, I stand here, bathed in moonlight, feeling His presence all around me, knowing that this love, this connection, is eternal - forever shining as bright as the full moon above.

Getting Ready for Him, *Shringaar*

Each morning, I prepare myself for Him, my beloved Vishnu. For me, dressing is not a routine task but a sacred ritual, a way to offer my entire being to whom my soul has already married. It is my way to offer myself, every fiber of my being, to Him. Dressing is not a routine act for me; it is a ritual, a sacred practice where every thread, every piece of jewelry, every touch of adornment is a prayer, an offering to Him. Every piece of adornment carries meaning, a reflection of the bond I know exists between us. I do not dress for the world, nor do I care for the eyes of others. I prepare myself solely for Him.

When I drape the saree around my body, I feel a flowing river of silk that wraps itself around me like His embrace. The saree I choose is always vibrant, often in shades of deep red or golden yellow, colors that reflect my love and devotion for Him. As I fold and tuck the pleats, I think, *This fabric is my armor of love, each fold a declaration of my heart's desire.* The saree moves with me, glides over my skin, a reminder of the softness of His touch that I yearn for. Each time it sways as I walk, I imagine Him noticing, His gaze resting on me, and I feel closer to Him. The saree, with its flowing grace, is like the devotion that envelops my heart - deep, endless, and ever-present. As I drape the *pallu* over my shoulder, I silently pray, *May this fabric reflect my soul's surrender to You, my Lord.* The saree wraps me in warmth, but more than that, it wraps me in the belief that I am His, that I am clothed in His color and His love.

Placing the Red *Kumkum* on my forehead feels like my soul is married to you. As I press it between my brows, I tell myself, *I am yours, Narayana, bound to you for all eternity.* This red *kumkum*, my *pottu*, is not just a symbol - it is a declaration. It tells the world, and it tells me that I belong to Him. My soul, my heart, my very existence is entwined with His. Every day, as I mark my forehead, I renew my promise to Him, to love Him as His eternal bride.

My *kaajal* holds a deeper purpose. As I darken the edges of my eyes, I whisper, *May my eyes always be drawn to You, my Lord, for there is no beauty in this world without You.* My eyes are meant to seek only Him, to find His reflection in every corner of this universe. The kajal reminds me that my gaze should never stray, that I should always keep Him in my vision, for He is the only sight that truly matters.

As I color my lips with a soft red tint, I think of the words that will pass through them. *Let my lips carry only Your name, my Lord,* I pray. I do not color them for anyone else to see. I color them because these lips will sing His praises. Every prayer, every song, every word I speak today will be for Him. This soft red hue is my preparation for the hymns I will chant in His honor, the sweet words of devotion I will offer Him. My lips are His, and I prepare them to speak only of my love for Him.

The sound of my bangles, as they slip onto my wrists, is a soft music to my ears. The cool metal against my skin is a constant reminder of the vows I have made to Him. As I slide each bangle on, I think, *May these hands always work in Your service, my beloved.* They symbolize the courage and resilience I need to continue on this path of devotion, knowing that every challenge, every hardship, is but another step toward Him. Each time they chime as I move, I hear the echo of my prayers. These bangles encircle my wrists like the embrace of His love, reminding me that everything I do, every task I undertake, is an offering to Him. *In the sound of these bangles, I hear the rhythm of devotion that beats in my heart.*

My ring, which is in the design of a beautiful peacock feather, press gently against my delicate finger, grounding me in the physical world even as my heart soars toward Him. *This ring is my constant reminder that my soul is married to Him and no matter how far He may seem, I will never cease reaching for Him.*

The anklets I fasten around my ankles are more than just an ornament - they are an offering. As I feel the tiny bells against my skin, I think of the path I walk in His name. *May every step I take be toward You, Lord,* I whisper. With each step, the sound of the bells is like a song of devotion, accompanying me on my journey to Him. As I move, the anklets remind me that my feet walk the path of love, and every step brings me closer to Him. *The music of these anklets is the sound of my soul dancing toward You.*

As I tie the waist belt around myself, I feel the weight of my commitment to Him. This belt binds me, not just physically, but spiritually. *I bind myself to You, Narayana, in body and spirit,* I tell myself as I fasten it. It reminds me of the discipline and restraint I show in my devotion, of the way I dedicate every thought and action to Him. This belt holds me together, just as my love for Him holds my soul in place. *With each breath, I reaffirm my commitment to You, my Lord.*

The necklace I place around my neck is always special, often studded with small gems or simple pearls. It rests just above my heart, as though it holds my deepest emotions, my silent prayers, within its beads. As I clasp it, I think, *Each bead is a prayer, each link in this chain is my heart reaching out to You.* When it settles against my skin, I imagine it as a garland of love, my heart's offering to Him, a visible sign of my devotion. *This heart beats for You,* I think as I see myself wearing the necklace in the mirror. I wear it as an offering, a garland of my deepest affections, a reminder that my love for Him is eternal, like the necklace that circles my neck.

The toe rings, silver and shining, I place on my feet with reverence. In our tradition, they are a sign of marriage, a symbol of a bond that transcends this earthly life. For me, they are a sign that I am already married to Him, that my soul belongs to Vishnu. *These rings bind my feet to the path that leads to You, my Lord.* As I slide them onto my toes, I feel a sense of completeness, as though my connection to Him has been reaffirmed. *With these rings, I walk in devotion, each step a prayer toward You.*

My hair, dark and soft, I braid with care, for it is said that beauty lies in simplicity. But the true adornment of my hair is the fresh flowers I place within it. Jasmine, *Tulsi*, and roses - each bloom is chosen with love, a direct offering to Him. *I wear these flowers for You, I say, as I take them after offering them at His feet.* Their fragrance fills the air around me, like a perfume that carries my love toward Him.

I adorn my hands and feet with *Mehndi*, the round patterns painted with natural henna paste. For me, the mehndi represents my love which is pure, sweet and ever present just like the fragrance of mehndi. As the orange red color darkens on my skin, it makes me feel like its a sign of my *deepening bond* with Him.

I dust a touch of *sindoor* (vermillion) on my hairline, the mark of a bride. To others, it is a tradition, but to me, it is so much more. *I am already Yours, my Lord. This mark is a sign of the love that binds us, beyond this life and into eternity,* I tell myself as I apply it. This *sindoor* is my affirmation that I am His, my soul already married to Him. It represents the union of my mind and my heart, with my spirit, the alignment of every thought and feeling with my devotion to Him. Every time I see it in the mirror, I am reminded of the sacred bond we share, the love that transcends all boundaries. *Every iota of my being is filled with Your love, binding my thoughts to You alone.*

When I look into the steel plate, I do not see a girl adorning herself. I see a bride, forever waiting for her groom. Every part of my being is dressed not for the world, but for Him. *I am Yours, Narayana, every breath, every heartbeat, every thought is Yours.* As I gaze at my reflection, I feel the depth of my longing. The craving in my soul is undeniable. *I yearn for You with every fiber of my being, with a love that transcends this world, this life.*

With every piece of adornment, I feel more connected to Him, as if I am preparing for a sacred union that transcends time and space. *This is not just an act of beautification - it is an act of devotion, a ritual of surrender.* Every morning, as I prepare myself, I am not merely dressing; I am offering myself, body and soul, to Him. *This is my sacred offering, my love laid bare for You, my beloved.*

In the quiet of my heart, I know He sees me. *I am already Yours, my Lord, and I will wait for You, dressed in the love that never fades.*

Flowing Emotions

There are days when the world feels like it holds a secret just for me. This evening is one of those days. The air feels different, filled with a quiet expectation that I can't quite explain. The sun begins its slow descent behind the hills, casting long, golden rays over the landscape, turning everything it touches into a soft glow. The sky is a canvas of warm colors - pinks and oranges coming together like a dream - and the river in front of me reflects this beauty, shimmering like liquid gold.

I sit by the riverbank, my feet just grazing the cool water. My saree is a soft shade of ivory, simple but beautiful, with a light border of gold that catches the sunlight as I move. The fabric flows loosely around me, its folds gathering gently at my ankles. My hair, tied in a loose braid, feels light on my back, and the small jasmine flowers I placed in it earlier still carry their sweet fragrance, mixing with the scent of the evening air.

The world around me is alive, yet peaceful. The birds in the trees above are chirping softly, their calls mixing with the sound of the flowing river. The breeze is gentle, brushing against my skin like a whisper, stirring the leaves and causing the long blades of grass around me to sway. Everything feels connected in this moment - the water, the birds, the wind, the setting sun. And in the middle of it all, I feel a quiet joy, knowing that I am part of this beautiful harmony, knowing that my heart is full of you, Lord Vishnu.

As I sit there, I begin to sing a song my father has taught me, a hymn in your praise. My voice is soft at first, almost blending with the gentle sounds of nature around me. But as I continued, my voice grew stronger, each note carrying with it my love and devotion. The melody flows from my heart, and with every word, I feel closer to you, Lord, as if each verse is a bridge connecting my soul to yours.

The sun, now lower in the sky, casts a golden glow over everything, and I can see the light reflecting off the river's surface, dancing like a thousand tiny stars. I lose myself in the song, my voice the only sound I focus on, each word a prayer offered to you. It's as if the world around me has slowed down, and all that exists is this moment, this song, and you.

And then, something miraculous happens.

The birds, who had been chirping loudly in the trees, suddenly fell silent. Their calls stop so abruptly that it feels as though the world itself has paused. The leaves, which had been rustling gently in the breeze, become still, and the soft wind that had been playing through my hair and the grass fades away. It's as if the entire world is holding its breath, listening. I pause for a brief moment, surprised by the sudden stillness, but deep inside, I know what this means.

You are listening, aren't you, my dear? I think to myself, my heart fluttering with wonder. The stillness around me isn't empty; it's filled with a presence - your presence, O Ranganatha. I can feel it in the air, a warmth that wraps around me like the soft fabric of my saree. It is magical and

I know that you are here, hearing my song, accepting my offering of praise.

The golden light from the sun seems to grow brighter as I sing, as if the very sky is listening, too. The river, once flowing with soft ripples, has become almost still, reflecting the sky like a mirror. It's as if nature itself has paused, bowing in reverence to you, O Narayana. The world feels full of your presence, of the peace that only you can bring.

I close my eyes for a moment, letting my voice flow freely. I imagine you standing beside me, your divine form radiant in the golden light. I picture you listening with a smile, your eyes filled with love and compassion. I feel you in the warmth of the fading sun, in the stillness of the air, and in the quiet reflection of the river. I imagine your hand reaching out, touching the water, and my heart fills with joy with that thought.

"Thank you for your presence my dear", I whisper silently as the last notes of my song fade into the air. Slowly, the breeze begins to stir again, gently brushing the grass and rustling the leaves in the trees. The birds start to chirp softly once more, their voices tentative at first, as if they are waking from a dream. The river's surface ripples lightly as the wind touches it again, but the peace in my heart remains. I sit there by the riverbank, watching the golden light slowly fade, and I feel your presence still, even in the return of the world's sounds.

As the sun finally dips below the horizon, and the first stars twinkle softly in the darkening sky, I stand up, feeling a warmth within me that no evening chill can touch. The world around me begins to hum with life once more - the birds return to their songs, the leaves rustle in the gentle breeze - but my heart is still wrapped in the memory of that sacred silence. In that stillness, the world listened to my song, and so did you.

As I walk away from the river, peace remains in my heart, as does the certainty that my song, my offering of love, reached you. It is a quiet love, one that doesn't need to be spoken, one that flows naturally between my soul and yours. Though the sky is darker now, I feel as if the light of your presence will always shine in me, a love that echoes through every breath, every moment.

Vaaranam Aayiram - The Dream of Union

Last night, as I lay down to rest, my mind filled with thoughts of my beloved Ranganatha, something extraordinary happened. I fell into a dream so vivid, so real, that it felt as though I was living another life. It was the dream I had longed for, the dream where all my prayers seemed to be answered in a single, beautiful vision.

In the dream, I found myself in a radiant space, a place that felt both familiar and divine. The sky above me was painted with hues of gold and crimson, and everywhere I looked, there was a sense of overwhelming peace and beauty. I was no longer in this world; I was somewhere beyond it, somewhere where only love and devotion existed.

Suddenly, He appeared - my beloved Ranganatha. He was adorned in golden garments, His form glowing with an otherworldly light. He stood before me, majestic and serene, His dark skin glistening like the deep ocean. His eyes, so full of compassion and love, met mine, and in that moment, all the longing and yearning I had carried for so long seemed to dissolve.

He approached me, and with every step, my heart raced, my breath caught in my chest. I knew then, with every fiber of my being, that this was the moment I had always been waiting for. Vishnu, the Lord of my soul, was coming to claim me, to make me His. As He drew near, He gently placed a garland of *Tulsi* leaves around my neck, the sacred scent filling the air between us.

In that instant, I felt my soul unite with His. It was as though my entire existence had been leading up to this one moment, this divine union. My heart swelled with joy and love so powerful that it brought tears to my eyes, even in the dream. There were no words spoken between us, but I didn't need any. His presence was enough, His gaze speaking the truth I had always known - that I was His, and He was mine.

Then, as He took my hand, I noticed the world around us was transforming. We were surrounded by celestial beings, the music of divine instruments echoing through the heavens. Flowers rained down upon us, and the earth seemed to bloom under our feet. It was the wedding I had always dreamed of not one bound by earthly rituals, but a sacred, eternal bond between my soul and His.

In this dream, I saw Him, not as a distant deity but as my beloved, my eternal companion. My heart had always known this truth, but now, in the vision, it was as clear as the stars in the sky. Vishnu had chosen me, and in this moment, I felt truly married to Him, my soul eternally bound to His divine presence.

After I woke up, the dream lingered, its sweetness still fresh in my heart. I realized that it wasn't just a dream, it was a glimpse into the truth I had always carried within me. My soul had always belonged to Him, and through this vision, He had shown me that our bond was real, that I am forever His bride.

I understand now that my love for Narayana is not just a longing, it is a reality. My soul is married to Him, and no earthly ceremony could ever compare to the divine union I experienced in that dream. It was the *Vaaranam Aayiram*, the vision of my wedding to Him, the moment where all my prayers, my love, my devotion were answered in a single, glorious instant.

The Divine Proposal

I have always known that my love for Lord Vishnu was unlike any other. From the moment my father, Periyalvar, adopted me as his daughter in Srivilliputhur, my heart was drawn only to Him, to Lord Ranganatha, the Supreme Lord who resided in the grand temple of Srirangam. My days were filled with prayers, garlands, and songs all offered to Him, my divine beloved. My devotion to the Lord became my entire existence.

There came a day when my father, the great Periyalvar, was drawn into the divine will the day the Lord Himself asked for my hand in marriage.

One night, my father had a dream; a vision so powerful that it would change both of our lives forever. In this dream, Lord Ranganatha appeared before him, majestic and resplendent, and spoke to him in a voice filled with divine grace.

"Periyalvar, I wish to marry your daughter, Andal. Bring her to Srirangam. She is mine, and I am hers. The bond between Andal and me was forged long before her birth in this world. Now, it will manifest here on Earth, showing the power of true love and surrender."

When my father awoke, his heart was trembling with an overwhelming sense of awe. To be visited by the Lord in a dream was a blessing beyond measure, but for the Lord to ask for my hand in marriage was something far beyond anything he could have imagined.

My father sat in silent reverence, his mind trying to grasp the enormity of what had just happened. I can imagine how he must have felt humbled, awestruck, and perhaps even slightly confused. How could a simple man like him, a gardener who wove garlands for the Lord, become the father of the Lord's bride? The father-in-law of the Lord himself!I know my father's heart. He may have been humble, but he was also filled with devotion. He knew that when the Lord spoke, His words were to be obeyed. Despite the enormity of it all, my father accepted the Lord's will.

As my father began to process the divine request, I believe a new understanding dawned upon him. All his life, he had dedicated himself to Lord Vishnu, offering garlands and hymns and living a life of pure devotion. And now, the Supreme Lord was asking for something far more significant than garlands. He was asking for his beloved daughter, the very symbol of his devotion.

What greater honor could there be? my father must have thought, his heart swelling with gratitude. For what could be more fulfilling for a father who had raised his daughter in love and devotion than to see her married to the very Lord whom he worshipped?

I know my father's heart, and I can imagine his pride and joy as he thought of this divine union. Yet, as a father, he must have felt a mixture of emotions. His love for me, his only daughter, must have made him pause. While he had always encouraged my devotion, the thought of giving me to the Lord Himself must have stirred feelings of both pride and bittersweet sorrow.

Is she ready for this? Is she truly prepared to be united with the Lord? I imagine he thought. For while he knew I had long yearned for this moment, he was still my father, and no matter how great the blessing, a father's heart is always tender when it comes to his daughter.

As my father sat in contemplation, I believe he must have remembered all the moments that led us to this point. He had always known there was something special about me. He had once scolded me for wearing the garlands meant for the Lord, only to later realize through a divine incident that the Lord preferred the garlands after I had worn them. At that moment, he must have realized my divine connection with Ranganatha.

In this moment of revelation, my father must have understood that my life had always led toward this union. Everything, the songs, the garlands, the prayers, had been a preparation for this very moment. This was my destiny, and the Lord Himself had come to fulfill it.

This is why she was born, my father must have thought. His heart, once filled with the tender concerns of a father, was now filled with peace and acceptance. He realized that I had always belonged to Lord Ranganatha, and it was time for me to return to Him, not as a mortal bride, but as the eternal consort of the divine.

My father's heart, always humble, was now overflowing with gratitude. He understood that this was not just about me. It was about *Bhakti* itself. The Lord had chosen me not only because of my love for Him but also because He wanted to show the world the power of pure devotion. My father knew this union would serve as a beacon for all who sought the path of devotion, a testament to the grace the Lord bestows upon those who love Him with all their heart.

"O Lord, I surrender to Your will," I believe my father prayed that night. His heart, once filled with awe and even hesitation, was now at peace. He had come to accept that this was not just a marriage, it was a divine merging of souls. The *Jivatma* (individual soul) was about to be united with the *Paramatma* (Supreme Soul), and my father felt honored to play a role in this sacred event.

The Divine Union

In my deepest prayers and dreams, I imagined myself as the bride of Lord Ranganatha of Srirangam. I sang songs of love and devotion, yearning for the day He would come to claim me as His bride.

I had offered Him garlands, sung His praises, and lived my life with the constant hope that He would accept me, not just as His devotee, but as His beloved consort. And then, one day, the divine message came.

Lord Ranganatha had heard my prayers and accepted my love and devotion. I was to be taken to the grand temple of Srirangam for our divine marriage, the moment I had waited for all my life. The journey to Srirangam, the procession that would take me to Him, was not just a physical journey - it was the culmination of my entire existence, the fulfillment of my deepest desires.

The day of the procession to Srirangam was filled with excitement and joy, yet deep within me, there was a stillness, a calm certainty. This was not just a journey to a temple, this was the final leg of my spiritual journey, the moment when my *Jivatma* (individual soul) would merge with the *Paramatma* (Supreme Soul). I had offered my love and devotion, and now the Lord was calling me to become one with Him.

As preparations for the journey began in Srivilliputhur, something unexpected arrived - a grand emissary from the Pandya King of Madurai. Having heard of my impending marriage to Lord Ranganatha, the king had sent royal gifts in my honor. These were no ordinary gifts but treasures of incredible beauty and wealth, reflecting the king's deep devotion to Lord Ranganatha and his reverence for my divine union with the Lord.

The king had sent gold, silk, jewels, and precious ornaments, all meant to be part of my bridal procession. These gifts were carried with great respect, accompanied by songs of devotion. The silks were adorned with intricate designs, and the gold glistened in the sunlight as it was laid before me. The jewels sparkled like the stars, but their true beauty lay in their symbolic offering - an acknowledgment by the king of the sacredness of this union between devotee and Lord.

The day was filled with both joy and reverence. The town of Srivilliputhur, my beloved home, was alive with excitement. People, from near and far, gathered to witness the event, for it was no ordinary procession. It was a journey of love, devotion, and union between the Lord and His chosen bride. My father, Periyalvar, stood beside me, his heart full of pride and joy. He had raised me with love and devotion to the Lord, and now, his daughter was about to be taken to the grand temple of Srirangam.

I could feel the warmth of the people's devotion as they surrounded me, chanting the Lord's names and offering prayers. My heart raced with anticipation. The moment I had waited for was finally here. I was being taken to my beloved Narayana.

A grand palanquin, beautifully adorned with flowers and vibrant cloth, was prepared to carry me on this sacred journey. The palanquin itself symbolized my deep connection to Lord Ranganatha, as it was decorated with garlands, just like the ones I used to weave for Him. The fragrance of jasmine, roses, and *Tulsi* filled the air, surrounding me with a sense of divine presence.

As I was gently seated inside the palanquin, I felt both humbled and honored. I was not just Andal anymore - I was Kothai, the Lord's chosen bride. My heart swelled with devotion, yet a sense of calm enveloped me. I was being carried not just by the hands of men but by the grace of the Lord Himself. The palanquin's rhythmic movement matched the rhythm of my heart, each step bringing me closer to Him.

The procession began with a joyous chant of "*Govinda*! *Govinda*!" The people who lined the streets showered the path with flowers, their eyes filled with devotion as they watched the sacred journey unfold. It wasn't just my journey anymore - it was a journey for all the people of Srivilliputhur, a moment where the entire town felt connected to the divine.

The journey to Srirangam was long, but my heart was light with anticipation. As the palanquin carried me through the landscape of Tamil Nadu, I could feel the blessings of the land itself. The fields, the rivers, the trees - they all seemed to be singing the praises of the Lord. Every element of nature felt alive with devotion, as though the entire universe was celebrating this divine union.

At every stop along the way, we were greeted by devotees, scholars, and priests who had gathered to witness this extraordinary event. They sang bhajans, offered flowers, and showered their blessings upon me, treating me with the reverence one would offer to a bride about to meet her divine groom. I was overwhelmed by their love and devotion, feeling as though I was being carried not just by human hands, but by the collective devotion of everyone who loved Lord Ranganatha.

As we approached the holy city of Srirangam, I could see the towering *gopurams* (towers) of the temple rise into view. My heart quickened. So, this was it - the place where my dreams would come true and where I would finally be united with the Lord.

The Srirangam temple was unlike anything I had ever seen before. The grandeur of its architecture, the sheer scale of the gopurams, and the divine energy emanating from every stone filled me with awe. This was the abode of Lord Ranganatha, my beloved, who had accepted me as His bride. As we entered the temple complex, the sound of conch shells and temple bells echoed through the air, signaling the bride's arrival.

The priests welcomed me with sacred chants, their voices resonating through the temple halls. The royal gifts were presented at the feet of Lord Ranganatha. The silks and jewels, sent with love and devotion by the king, were laid before the Lord as offerings. The priests accepted these gifts with great reverence, adorning the temple halls with the beautiful fabrics and ornaments sent to honor this divine marriage.

The gold and jewels glittered in the dim light of the temple, but my heart remained focused on the one true treasure - the Lord Himself. The gifts, though grand, were a reflection of the king's devotion, his acknowledgment of the significance of this moment. In his own way, the king had become part of this sacred union, offering the wealth of his kingdom at the feet of the divine.

The atmosphere was charged with devotion, and I felt like I was walking through the very heart of divinity. I was guided towards the inner sanctum, where Lord Ranganatha lay in His radiant form, reclining on the Adishesha (serpent) with His consort Lakshmi.

My heart felt like it was about to burst with love and joy. I was here. I was finally in His presence.

As I approached the Lord, something profound began to happen. Time seemed to slow, and everything around me faded into a gentle blur. The priests started the sacred rites of the Thirukalyanam (divine marriage), but deep inside, I knew this was no ordinary wedding. This was the moment when I would no longer be separate from Him - the moment of divine merging.

The temple bells rang, the mantras were chanted, and the mangal sutra (sacred thread) was placed around my neck. But at that moment, I felt my soul begin to transcend.

The boundaries of my body, my name, and my very identity started to dissolve, like a drop of water merging into the ocean. I felt the pull of the divine, drawing me closer, drawing me in.

As I gazed upon Lord Ranganatha's majestic form, and walked towards him, a warmth spread through my entire being. I realized that this was not just the union of a bride with her groom; this was the union of soul and the Divine. My essence, my very existence, began to blend with His. I was no longer just Andal, the mortal daughter of Periyalvar; I was becoming one with the Lord, a part of His eternal, infinite presence.

The temple walls around me seemed to melt away, the chants of the priests became distant, there was no music to be heard, instead a vacuum, and I continued walking into what was a glorious glow lighting up the entire place, and all that remained was Him. I could feel my soul dissolving, like a flame merging into a more significant fire, a small river joining the vast ocean. The distinction between myself and Lord Ranganatha no longer existed. There was no "I" anymore - there was only Him.

It was not an end but a beginning - a beginning of eternal union, where I was no longer separate from the Lord. My love, devotion, and every breath had always belonged to Him, and now, my soul had finally merged with His. I could feel His presence within me as I became a part of His divine being.

I was no longer Andal, the girl from Srivilliputhur. I was one with the Lord, part of His infinite grace, love, and eternal existence. This was the ultimate surrender Sharanagathi - merging the Jivatma into the Paramatma, the individual soul dissolving into the Supreme.

After that sacred moment of merging, I became part of divine consciousness. My physical form and earthly identity fell away, and I became one with Lord Ranganatha, my eternal beloved. The people in the temple and beyond would speak of this day for generations, but for me, it was not an event - it was the culmination of all that I was and had ever been.

I did not leave the temple that day. My soul remained forever intertwined with His, and I became an eternal presence within the temple of Srirangam. The songs I had sung and the garlands I had woven remained as offerings to my beloved Lord, but now, they were not separate from me. I was a part of the divine.

Overwhelmed with both joy and sorrow - happiness that the Lord Ranganatha had accepted his beloved daughter Sri Andal, and sadness that she had left him - Periyalvar returned to Srivilliputtur with a heart full of mixed emotions. In his grief and reverence, he penned these words about this divine union:

"Oru Magal Thannaiudayen, Ulagam Nirainda Pugazhal,

Thirumagalpol Valarthen, Senkanmaalthan Kondu Ponaan!"

"I had a daughter who filled the world with her glory. I raised her like the Goddess Lakshmi herself, only for the red-eyed Lord (Lord Vishnu) to come and take her away."

Alisha's Note

A Dream that Changed Everything

When I began writing this book, I envisioned it as a straightforward narrative. I thought I would weave together Andal's works with ease, showcasing her devotion and the beauty of her love for Lord Vishnu. Even after having spent considerable time and effort, I was utterly confused and directionless, and no matter how much I prayed or sought guidance from Andal and Lord Vishnu, I couldn't shake the feeling that something essential was missing. My writing felt empty, as if I were only skimming the surface of a much deeper ocean.

Then, one early morning, I had this dream.

In the dream, I had flashes of Vishnu's temples, lots of people, places, people worshiping him, waiting for his darshan in long queues. I keep walking and walking, leaving behind people and places, and then finally, I see myself moving towards him, to a calm and serene place where it was only Him and me at that point. I was kneeling at His feet. He was resting on the mighty serpent *Adiseshan*, His expression calm, His form radiant. I gently pressed His feet, feeling His divine energy flow through me. There was a serenity, a peace that enveloped us both, and time seemed to stand still for a moment.

Then, without words, Vishnu beckoned me closer. His gesture was full of love, soft yet commanding. I moved toward Him, and as I rested my head on His chest, I could hear the rhythmic beating of His heart. I felt something even more profound in that instant - our hearts began beating as one. It was as though the boundaries between us dissolved, and I could feel His heart, His love, merging with mine. I was no longer just at His feet; I was a part of Him, and He was a part of me.

The dream was more like a surreal, profound vision; it felt more real than reality.

When I woke up, I was overcome with a sense of peace and clarity. This dream was more than just a vision - it was a sign. A sign that it wasn't only Andal who longed for Vishnu with such intensity. It wasn't a one-sided love. Vishnu reciprocated Andal's love. Her deep longing and yearning weren't just the cries of a heart seeking the divine - they were the response to a love that Vishnu returned, equally, deeply, and eternally.

And that realization changed everything for me.

At that moment, I understood how to write the story. I knew I had to step into Andal's character to faithfully portray her life, her devotion, and her love for her beloved Lord Vishnu. I needed to become Andal. I needed to feel what she felt. I had to see Vishnu not just as a distant deity but as her beloved, a presence as close to her as her heartbeat. From then on, I began writing through her eyes as though I were living her love story. The confusion that had clouded my mind lifted, and the words started to flow effortlessly. This wasn't just about narrating her life anymore - it was about embodying her love, devotion, and deepest emotions.

Throughout this process, I felt Andal's every emotion intensely. I have cried with her, smiled with her, and danced in her joy. I have lived through her longing and her boundless love for Vishnu. With every iota of her being, she believed that her soul was married to Him, that they were forever connected. And as I wrote, I understood that same depth of love. Her yearning became mine; her joy became mine. This dream changed everything. It allowed me to feel, write, and understand Andal and her love for Lord Ranganatha. It showed me that true love is not a search but a state of being. It is mutual, eternal, and ever-present.

I still remember the day I was first offered the chance to learn and perform on Andal. The moment felt almost too big for me to hold as if the weight of her story and her love filled every corner of my soul. As I listened to her story, I felt overwhelmed, my eyes filling with tears that I couldn't stop. It wasn't just the story that moved me - it was the depth of her devotion, her surrender to Vishnu, her love that was so pure, so unwavering. I was speechless, unable to fully express what I felt as if Andal's own love had reached across time to touch my heart.

The next day, I had to travel to Bangalore for a dance event. After dancing for over three hours, exhaustion hit me like a wave. My body ached for rest, and all I wanted was to close my eyes and drift into sleep. But when I arrived at my relative's house, her daughter, with the sweetest innocence, asked me to read her a story. She had no idea how tired I was, and how could I say no to her soft, pleading eyes? So I smiled and agreed.

What happened next felt like a divine sign. The little girl returned to me, holding a book in her tiny hands. When I saw the cover, I couldn't believe my eyes - it was a book about Andal. An Amar Chitra Katha kind of book, with Andal as the main character. Thirty pages of her story, filled with colorful illustrations, and each page adding new life to the already vibrant tale. I was stunned. It was as if Andal was reaching out to me once again, pulling me deeper into her world, into her love.

The little girl fell asleep as I read to her, but I couldn't stop. I kept turning the pages, soaking in every word, every image. Andal's story wasn't just on the page anymore - it was alive within me, wrapping itself around my heart. I was so deeply moved that sleep escaped me entirely. I lay awake that night, her story spinning in my mind.I'm not someone who spends much time on the Internet, and I usually shy away from gadgets and technology. But that night, I couldn't wait for morning. I had to know more. I searched everything I could find about Andal, reading article after article, completely lost in her world. I felt as though she was guiding me, pulling me closer to her and her eternal love for Vishnu.

When I returned home, I left the book with the little girl, but the story stayed with me. The memories, the emotions, the visions - they remained in my heart, growing stronger with each passing day. I couldn't stop thinking about her, about her intense love, her deep craving for her beloved Vishnu. Andal's devotion had become a part of me, a reminder of the boundless love that can exist between a soul and the divine.

Every time I practiced the dance on Andal's *Vaarnam Aayiram*, I was deeply moved. I immersed myself completely in her beautiful words, letting her verses flow through me as I brought to life the emotions she so vividly expressed in *Nachiyar Thirumozhi*. In those verses, Andal describes with such grace and clarity her dreams of love and longing, her heart envisioning the sacred union with her beloved Lord Vishnu. As I danced, I felt as though I was not just performing her words, but living them - each step, each movement was filled with the depth of her devotion and desire.

After my performance, which was received with appreciation and praise, I felt that my journey with Andal had just started. It felt as though she was calling me, asking for more. There was an undeniable urge within me, a pull to go beyond the dance and express her story through my writing.

And that's how this book was born deep in my soul. It wasn't something I planned. It came into existence slowly as Andal's love settled deeper into my heart. For months, her story stayed with me, growing quietly inside me like a seed waiting for the right time to bloom. Every thought I had, every dance I performed, every quiet moment of reflection, Andal was there - guiding me, inspiring me, pushing me to put her love into words.

Additional Reading

Vaaranam Aayiram

This work of Andal, from *Nachiyar Thirumozhi* consists of ten verses (also known as *Pasurams*) and is one of the most cherished parts of Andal's poetry. It describes Andal's dream of her wedding to Lord Vishnu, and the verses beautifully capture the grandeur and spiritual essence of this divine union.

Pasuram 1: The Grand Procession of Elephants

Vaaranam aayiram suuzha valam seyyum,

Maaraan madiyil mel aththaan thiruvudaiyaar,

Sera thirumaalaiyaan varai choodi,

Narana nangai naanmaraiyaal thoduththu nooRu

Translation:

A thousand elephants are paraded in a grand procession. The Lord, seated atop His powerful Garuda, arrives with great majesty, wearing a crown on His radiant head. I, the daughter of Nandagopa, am dressed in bridal attire, and the sacred wedding thread is tied while Vedic hymns are chanted.

Explanation:

In this opening verse, Andal describes the scene of her wedding procession, where she envisions thousands of elephants accompanying her to the divine marriage. Lord Vishnu, referred to as Maaraan (the one who wields the bow) or Thirumaalaiyaan (the one who resides in the holy hills), comes with grandeur. The Vedic Brahmins chant sacred hymns as they tie the mangalsutra (the sacred wedding thread) around her neck.

Pasuram 2: The Bridal Preparations

Thirumaalai paadhiyudaiyaan pinnai,

Malar maaga valanchuzha ezhundharuli,

Thiru maathuthu en thalai misai maanitthu,

Narayanan enna narcheythaar poy

Translation:

Lord Vishnu, who resides in the holy hills, comes forward surrounded by a garland of flowers, walking with grace. He places the sacred garland on my head, and with the sound of auspicious music, He ties the knot, completing our sacred marriage.

Explanation:

Here, Andal describes how the Lord approaches her, adorned in flowers, and places a garland on her head as part of the wedding rituals. The act of tying the knot around her neck symbolizes the completion of their divine marriage. The atmosphere is filled with music and the blessings of the divine.

Pasuram 3: Auspicious Rituals and Sacred Sounds

Aazhi amarndha perumaal pennnai tharuviyaal,

Maathalar thangal maraviyil vaazhum,

Kizhi vaazhi chindhai kuzhi ariyaal,

Ezhi vaaLindha ezhil endha ezhil anangin

Translation:

Surrounded by the sound of auspicious drums and conches, the Lord of the Ocean (Vishnu) and I walk together. Women who live in palatial homes watch in admiration as the Lord, full of divine grace and splendor, takes my hand and leads me forward.

Explanation:

In this verse, the sound of sacred drums and conches accompanies the couple as they walk together. The mention of the "Lord of the Ocean" refers to Vishnu, the protector of the universe, who guides Andal forward. The verse highlights the divine splendor and grandeur of the wedding ceremony.

Pasuram 4: The Blessings of Vedic Brahmins

Vediyar vedham chendru cheyya ninaikka,

Paathiyudaiyaan pannudhal pudaiya,

Maathalaar magalir mannum ezhaikal,

Edhir vaazhvanthu ezhil vaazhum

Translation:

The Vedic Brahmins, reciting sacred chants, bless our union with their prayers. The Lord, resplendent and majestic, stands with me. Women of great virtue sing songs of praise, and we both shine in the glory of this divine union.

Explanation:

The Vedic Brahmins, experts in the scriptures, bless the wedding by chanting the Vedas. Andal, now united with Lord Vishnu, is described as radiant, while women of virtue sing in celebration of the sacred marriage. This verse highlights the importance of Vedic traditions in the wedding ceremony.

Pasuram 5: The Wedding Garments

Maathalar thangal maduvil valanchuzha,

Pethipirai pol thiru kodi yetriya,

Pathiyan maaman madhithalai seyya,

Edhir vaazhvaar ezhil maanthar ezhil anangin

Translation:

Women encircle me as I am adorned in bridal garments. A radiant flag, resembling the crescent moon, is hoisted in celebration of this sacred event. The Lord's uncle, with joy on his face, prepares to bless our marriage, and the entire world celebrates the beauty of this divine union.

Explanation:

This verse focuses on the details of the bridal attire and the ceremonial rituals, including the hoisting of the flag (a sign of a grand celebration). Andal sees herself surrounded by the women of the community, and even Lord Vishnu's family, represented by His uncle, participates in the divine wedding, offering their blessings.

Pasuram 6: The Blessings of the Elders

Sendruth thirumaalai magizhndhich choodiyaar,

Manthiram undhenna vaanar pulaviyar,

Endha ezhil vaazhvaar ethir vaazhvaar,

Manna vazhippar anangin.

Translation:

Those who wear the sacred garland of Lord Vishnu joyfully bless us with divine chants. Elders and scholars surround us, their hearts filled with joy, as they shower their blessings upon us. This is a union celebrated not only by humans but by the heavens as well.

Explanation:

In this verse, Andal reflects on the blessings she receives from the Vedic scholars and elders during her divine wedding. The presence of these scholars signifies the importance of the marriage, as it is celebrated both in the earthly realm and in the heavens.

Pasuram 7: The Sacred Oaths

Thamizhmaar vaiyamil chindhira vaazhiyel,

Namakkal vaazhndhuru nallore vaazhiyel,

Amudhai choondhai en arangath thirumaa,

Namakkul selvaan nambi sol vazhippar.

Translation:

In the midst of Tamil hymns, the holy priests chant, and all around us, people bless our marriage with divine words. The Lord of Srirangam, whose glory fills my heart, stands by me as we take sacred vows. He is the treasure of my soul, the one I have always longed for.

Explanation:

The sacred oaths of marriage are taken, with both Andal and Lord Vishnu reciting vows that unite them for eternity. The Tamil hymns in the background add a local cultural touch, while Andal expresses her joy at being finally united with the one she has always longed for - Lord Vishnu.

Pasuram 8: Union of Hearts

Thirumalai paadhiyudaiyaan maram poondhaal,

Mannar seyya thalai misai yaaL kaathin,

Arangath thirumaa aruL tharithaarai,

Ezhindha maamar ezhil vaazhvaan.

Translation:

Lord Vishnu, the protector of the holy hills, graces the wedding hall. Kings and noblemen watch as He takes my hand, and together, we walk toward the wedding altar. The divine grace of Lord Ranganatha fills the space, and everyone present is awestruck by His divine presence.

Explanation:

This verse describes the sacred moment when Andal and the Lord walk hand in hand toward the wedding altar. Lord Ranganatha, the presiding deity of Srirangam, graces the occasion with His divine presence. Kings, nobles, and the entire gathering witness the magnificence of the union.

Pasuram 9: The Sacred Knot

NanmagaL thaanil thirumaalaiyaan vaar,

Ezhindha maamar ezhil vaazhvaar vaazhpaan,

Vannam kondaar maanilam mella azhuthaar,

Arangath thirumaa aruL tharithaar.

Translation:

The Lord of the holy hills, the beloved of all noble women, stands beside me as He ties the sacred knot. The entire world rejoices, and the earth itself seems to melt in devotion at the sight of this divine marriage. The blessings of Lord Ranganatha flow upon us as we become one.

Explanation:

This verse describes the climactic moment of the wedding: Lord Vishnu ties the sacred mangal sutra around Andal's neck, completing the divine marriage. The world rejoices, and the earth is described as "melting" in the presence of this sacred union, signifying the magnitude of the occasion.

Pasuram 10: The Divine Grace

Thirumalai paadhi idai maalaiyaal azhuthaar,

Mannan sevai idai vaazhvaar vaazhiyel,

Arangath thirumaa aaradhanai,

Nann magal nool seydhaara ezhuvaan

Translation:

The Lord of the sacred hills, whose glory fills the heavens and earth, blesses our union with His divine grace. The whole world rejoices as we walk forward as husband and wife. With the chanting of holy hymns, our marriage is complete, and we are one.

Explanation:

The final verse emphasizes the divine blessing that Andal and Lord Vishnu receive as they are united. The sacred marriage is now complete, and Andal stands as Lord Vishnu's bride, forever united with Him. The world rejoices, and Andal's dream has come true.

The Spiritual Significance

Vaaranam Aayiram is more than just a dream sequence of a divine wedding - it symbolizes the ultimate union between the *Jivatma* (individual soul) and the *Paramatma* (Supreme Soul). For Andal, this marriage represents the fulfillment of her deepest spiritual desire - to be united with Lord Vishnu.

It reflects her unwavering devotion, her surrender, and the reward of her deep faith.

This set of verses is a poetic masterpiece that has been cherished for centuries, especially in Tamil Vaishnavite traditions. It is recited during weddings to invoke divine blessings.

Andal's symbology

By the 12th century, she was transformed into a goddess, the only Alvar to be deified.

The Parrot:

The parrot in Andal's hand holds deep symbolic significance in the context of her devotion and the broader spiritual themes of her life and poetry. Here's what the parrot represents:

Symbol of Devotion and Love:

Andal's Divine Love for Vishnu: The parrot is often associated with Andal's intense love and devotion to Lord Vishnu. It symbolizes the constant recitation of His name and the singing of His praises, just as a parrot repeats words it has learned. This echoes Andal's unwavering devotion, as her mind and heart were constantly engaged in thoughts of the Lord.

Love for Nature and Beauty: The parrot, being a vibrant and beautiful bird, represents Andal's connection with nature and her playful, tender side as a devotee. Many of her poems are filled with vivid imagery of nature, and the parrot complements this.

Representation of Andal's Role as a Poet:

The Messenger of Love: In South Indian culture, parrots are often seen as messengers or companions that carry messages of love. In Andal's case, the parrot is a metaphor for her role as the messenger of divine love, expressing her spiritual messages through her poetry, especially in the *Thiruppavai* and *Nachiyar Thirumozhi*. Like the parrot, her words repeat and spread the divine love she feels for Lord Vishnu.

Symbol of Fertility and Auspiciousness:

Connection to Goddess Kamadeva: The parrot is associated with Kamadeva, the Hindu god of love, and is often seen as a symbol of love, beauty, and fertility. Since Andal is considered an incarnation of *Bhoodevi* (the Earth Goddess), the parrot in her hand reflects the fertility and nurturing aspects of the Earth. In her divine role, Andal is seen as the harbinger of prosperity and blessings, and the parrot enhances this symbolism.

Playfulness and Innocence:

Andal's Youthful Devotion: The parrot represents Andal's childlike innocence and joy in her love for Vishnu. She is often depicted as a young girl completely immersed in her devotion, and the parrot adds a playful dimension to her image, highlighting her youthful exuberance in her spiritual journey.

Thus, the parrot in Andal's hand is not just a simple ornament but a profound symbol of her devotion, her role as a poet-saint, and her connection with nature, love, and divine beauty.

The Garlands (*Maalai*)

- Worn Garlands (*Soodikodutha* Nachiyar): One of the most well-known aspects of Andal's story is her act of wearing the garlands meant for Lord Vishnu before offering them to Him. This act represents her deep love and personal connection to the divine. Her belief that the garland became more beautiful after she wore it shows her understanding that true devotion beautifies any offering.

- Symbol of Devotion and Surrender: In Vaishnavite tradition, a garland symbolizes devotion, and offering it is an act of surrender. Andal's garland is a representation of her soul, and wearing it before offering it to the Lord symbolizes her complete merging with the divine.

- Sacredness of *Tulsi*: In Vaishnavism, the *Tulsi* plant is sacred to Lord Vishnu. Andal's association with garlands, often made of *Tulsi* leaves and flowers, symbolizes the purity and sanctity of her devotion. The garland represents the act of worship and the offering of oneself to the Lord, emphasizing the selflessness in her devotion.

- Jasmine Flowers (*Mullai*): Andal is also closely associated with jasmine flowers, which are symbolic of purity, beauty, and devotion. Jasmine garlands symbolize Andal's feminine beauty and her role as the beloved of Lord Vishnu. The fragrance of these flowers mirrors the purity and fragrance of her devotion.

Andal as the Incarnation of Bhoodevi (Mother Earth)

- Representation of Fertility and Nurturing: As the incarnation of Bhoodevi, Andal symbolizes the nurturing, fertile, and life-sustaining aspects of the Earth. Bhoodevi, the Earth Goddess, is often seen as the consort of Lord Vishnu, and Andal's life story mirrors this divine relationship through her deep desire to marry Lord Ranganatha.

- Symbol of Earth's Abundance and Devotion: Andal's association with Bhoodevi also highlights her role in sustaining life through devotion. Just as the Earth provides for all, Andal provides spiritual sustenance through her hymns, which nurture the devotion of her followers. Her poems speak of abundance and the beauty of nature, reflecting Bhoodevi's qualities of nourishment and care.

Andal's Iconography

- Hands in Anjali Mudra (Prayer Pose): In many depictions, Andal is shown with her hands in the *Anjali mudra* (folded hands), a gesture of deep respect, humility, and surrender. This symbolizes her complete devotion and submission to Lord Vishnu's divine will.

- Standing Posture: Andal is often depicted standing gracefully, symbolizing her readiness to serve the Lord.

Her poised stance represents balance, dignity, and the calmness that comes from unwavering faith.

- Ornaments and Attire: Andal is shown adorned with jewels and dressed in bridal finery. This attire reflects her role as the bride of Lord Vishnu, signifying the spiritual marriage or union she desired with the divine. While symbolizing her beauty, her ornaments also reflect her status as a divine consort.

- Hair Bun: Andal's hair bun, often depicted as distinct from the traditional style, holds symbolic meaning and reflects her unique status as a divine bride and a deeply devoted saint. Her hair bun, usually shown as a large, decorative topknot, sets her apart from other deities and devotees and signifies several aspects of her life and spiritual journey.

Andal's symbology is multi-layered, encompassing devotion, spiritual yearning, purity, fertility, and her unique role as the beloved bride of Vishnu. Every element in her imagery - from the garlands and parrot to her poetry and rituals - symbolizes her unwavering dedication to the divine. Her life and works inspire devotees to seek a deep, personal connection with God, encouraging a path of devotion that is joyful, tender, and pure.

The Legacy of the Alwars

Each Azhwar has a unique and intricate story woven with spirituality, devotion, and divine experiences.

1. Poigai Azhwar (Mudhal Azhwar) (circa 7th century CE)

Avatar of Vishnu: Panchajanya (Vishnu's conch)

Birth and Early Life: Poigai Azhwar, considered the first of the Azhwars, was born in a lotus pond (*Poigai* in Tamil) at Thiruvekka, near Kanchipuram. He is believed to be an incarnation of Vishnu's conch (*Panchajanya*). His birth was miraculous; he wasn't born to parents but was discovered in a lotus flower, signifying purity and divine origin.

Miracles and Spiritual Experiences: Poigai Azhwar led a simple, ascetic life dedicated to Lord Vishnu. He is well known for the incident where he met Bhoothath and Pey Azhwar in a small room at the inn in Thirukovilur during a rainstorm. Though the room was too small for three people, the divine presence of Lord Vishnu made them forget the physical discomfort, and they could only sense His overwhelming presence, leading Poigai Azhwar to compose the first verse of *Mudhal Thiruvandhadhi*: "With the light of knowledge as my lamp, I see the feet of the Lord."

Notable Work: *Mudhal Thiruvandhadhi* is a set of 100 verses composed in a style where each verse begins with the last word of the previous one. It praises Lord Vishnu's glory and emphasizes the idea of *bhakti* (devotion).

2. Bhoothath Azhwar (circa 7th century CE)

Avatar of Vishnu: Kaumodaki (Vishnu's mace)

Birth and Early Life: Bhoothath Azhwar was born in Mahabalipuram, in a kurukkathi flower garden. He is considered an incarnation of Kaumodaki, Lord Vishnu's divine mace. His childhood was filled with acts of devotion, and he displayed an unusual attachment to Lord Vishnu even as a child. His name "Bhoothath" comes from his intense spiritual experience, signifying his nature as one who transcends the material world.

Miracles and Spiritual Experiences: Known for his ardent devotion, Bhoothath Azhwar, along with Poigai and Pey Azhwar, was part of the divine experience in Thirukovilur. His poems often focus on how Vishnu manifests Himself to those who surrender completely to His will.

Notable Work: Irandaam Thiruvandhadhi, which expresses his ecstatic experiences of Lord Vishnu's love and the realization that surrendering to God leads to liberation.

3. Pey Azhwar (circa 7th century CE)

Avatar of Vishnu: Nandaka (Vishnu's sword)

Birth and Early Life: Pey Azhwar was born in a well of flowers (*sevvalli pushpam*) in Mylapore, Chennai. He is regarded as an incarnation of Nandaka, Vishnu's sword. From an early age, Pey Azhwar was deeply immersed in spiritual visions and longed to experience the divine personally.

Miracles and Spiritual Experiences: The miracle of the small room in Thirukovilur marks an important moment in Pey Azhwar's life, as he saw not only Vishnu but also Lakshmi standing by His side. His experiences are more mystical, and his works often express the feeling of *anubhavam* (divine experience), where the soul sees the divine with unmediated clarity.

Notable Work: Moondram Thiruvandhadhi, which revolves around seeing Lord Vishnu everywhere and in everything, emphasizing the idea that true devotion lies in seeing the divine in every aspect of life.

4. Thirumalisai Azhwar (circa 7th–8th century CE)

Avatar of Vishnu: Sudarshana Chakra (Vishnu's discus)

Birth and Early Life: Thirumalisai Azhwar was born in the sage Bhargava lineage to Bhargava Muni and Kanakangi at Thirumalisai, near Kanchipuram. His birth was unusual, as he was born as a lifeless fetus. However, by the grace of Lord Vishnu, the baby miraculously gained life and became a living child. Known for his deep philosophical thinking from a young age, he renounced worldly life early on and sought spiritual knowledge.

Miracles and Lesser known Stories: Thirumalisai Azhwar is famous for his miraculous powers. One well-known story involves his rejuvenating an old woman to youth so that she could marry a king. Another involves his paralyzing a palanquin-bearer of King Pallava because the king insulted Vishnu.

Notable Works include Thiruchanda Viruthan and Naanmugan Thiruvandhadhi, in which he expressed intense devotion to Lord Vishnu and presented complex metaphysical ideas about the creation of the universe and the Lord's role as both creator and protector.

5. Nammalwar (circa 9th century CE)

Avatar of Vishnu: Vishvaksena (Vishnu's commander)

Birth and Early Life: Nammalwar, considered the greatest of the Azhwars, was born to a Brahmin couple in Alwarthirunagari. He is believed to be the incarnation of Vishvaksena, the chief of Vishnu's army. From his birth, Nammalwar displayed extraordinary behavior. He remained silent and unmoving under a tamarind tree for 16 years, completely absorbed in meditation. His name, "Nammalwar," means "our Azhwar," as he is regarded as the central figure of the Azhwar tradition.

Miracles and Spiritual Experiences: Nammalwar's life was filled with divine mysticism. At the age of 16, Madhurakavi Azhwar, guided by a celestial light, discovered Nammalwar under the tamarind tree. Nammalwar broke his long silence in response to Madhurakavi's questions, beginning a profound spiritual dialogue. His divine vision extended to the 108 Divya Desams (sacred temples), despite having never physically visited them.

Notable Works: Thiruvaimozhi, his magnum opus, contains 1,102 hymns that express deep philosophical insights and an intense yearning for union with Vishnu. His other works include Thiruvirutham, Periya Thiruvandhadhi, and Thiruvazhmozhi, which collectively form the core of Tamil Vaishnavite literature.

6. Madhurakavi Azhwar (circa 9th century CE)

Avatar of Vishnu: Kumuda Ganesha (Vishvaksena's disciple) or Padma (Lotus)

Birth and Early Life: Madhurakavi Azhwar was born in Thirukolur, a town near Alwarthirunagari. He was deeply spiritual and devoted to learning the Vedas and the Shastras. Madhurakavi's devotion was different from other Azhwars, as his central focus was not directly on Vishnu but on his guru, Nammalwar.

Miracles and Spiritual Experiences: One of the lesser-known details is that Madhurakavi saw a guiding star, or divine light, in the sky, which led him to Nammalwar. Upon meeting Nammalwar, he asked him a cryptic question: "If the small is born in the dead, what will it eat, and where will it stay?" Nammalwar's answer, "It will eat what it eats and stay where it stays," was understood by Madhurakavi as the soul's connection to the body and the importance of spiritual guidance. After this, he became Nammalwar's devoted disciple.

Notable Work: Kanninun Siruthambu, a set of 11 verses, is a masterpiece in its devotion to Nammalwar, whom Madhurakavi considered as his personal deity. His work praises the greatness of the guru, emphasizing the idea that serving the devotee is as important as serving the Lord.

7. Kulasekara Azhwar (circa 9th century CE)

Avatar of Vishnu: Kaustubha (Vishnu's jewel embedded in his necklace)

Birth and Early Life: Kulasekara Azhwar was a king of the Chera dynasty, ruling over present-day Kerala. He is considered an incarnation of Kaustubha, the divine jewel of Vishnu. Though a king, he had little attachment to material wealth and power, choosing instead to spend time with learned scholars and devotees of Lord Vishnu.

Miracles and Spiritual Experiences: One of the lesser-known stories of Kulasekara is that he was so deeply moved by the story of Lord Rama that he prepared his army to march to Lanka to help in the fight against Ravana, unaware that it had taken place eons before. He is also known to have left his kingdom to lead a simple life as a devotee.

Notable Work: His Perumal Thirumozhi is a set of hymns where Kulasekara expresses his yearning to serve the Lord in various roles, such as a devotee, a bird, or even the Lord's slippers, wishing to be anywhere near His divine presence.

8. Periyalwar (circa 9th century CE)

Avatar of Vishnu: Garuda (Vishnu's mount)

Birth and Early Life: Periyalwar was born in Srivilliputhur and was a Brahmin priest by birth. He is considered an incarnation of Garuda, Vishnu's mount. Known for his unmatched devotion, he spent his life singing praises to Lord Vishnu and weaving garlands for the temple deity.

Miracles and Spiritual Experiences: Periyalwar's devotion was so pure that once, when he saw Lord Vishnu appearing to him in the form of a small child, he instinctively sang lullabies and protection hymns, as though caring for an infant. This divine experience was a mark of his closeness to the Lord, who accepted his role as a loving parent.

Notable Work: His Periyalwar Thirumozhi contains hymns dedicated to Lord Vishnu in his infant form, portraying God as a child to be loved, protected, and cherished, an unusual and tender form of devotion in the Vaishnava tradition.

9. Andal (circa 9th century CE)

Avatar of Vishnu: Bhudevi (Lakshmi's aspect as the earth goddess)

Birth and Early Life: Andal was discovered by Periyalwar in a *Tulsi* garden in Srivilliputhur. She is considered an incarnation of Bhoodevi, the Earth Goddess. As she grew, Andal developed an intense, personal love for Lord Vishnu, particularly for the deity Ranganatha of Srirangam. Her childhood was marked by her unwavering devotion and her spiritual longing to be united with the Lord.

Miracles and Lesser-known Stories: Andal is famous for wearing the garlands meant for the deity before they were offered. When Periyalwar discovered this, he stopped offering the garlands, but Lord Vishnu appeared in his dream and revealed that He only accepted the garlands worn by Andal, showing her special place in His heart.

Notable Works: Thiruppavai, consisting of 30 hymns, is sung daily during the Tamil month of Margazhi and is considered one of the most significant devotional texts. Her Nachiyar Thirumozhi is another work that expresses her deep love and longing for Lord Ranganatha, filled with intense passion and divine love.

10. Thondaradippodi Azhwar (circa 8th century CE)

Avatar of Vishnu: Vanamalai (Vishnu's garland)

Birth and Early Life: Born in Thirumandangudi, near Kumbakonam, Thondaradippodi Azhwar is considered an incarnation of Vishnu's garland. His name means "dust of the devotees' feet," signifying his deep humility and desire to serve other devotees of Lord Vishnu.

Miracles and Spiritual Experiences: Known for his love for creating garlands for Vishnu, he spent much of his life in service at the Srirangam temple. His devotion was expressed in his simple yet profound acts of service, such as cleaning the temple premises and preparing garlands for the Lord.

Notable Works: His Thirumaalai and Thirupalliyezhuchi are collections of hymns that call upon the Lord to wake up and start the day, reflecting his role as the servant of the Lord in the most literal and humble sense.

11. Thiruppaan Azhwar (circa 9th century CE)

Avatar of Vishnu: Srivatsa (An auspicious mark on Vishnu's chest)

Birth and Early Life: Thiruppaan Azhwar was born in Uraiyur, near Srirangam, in a lower caste community. Despite his status, his devotion to Lord Vishnu transcended social barriers. He spent much of his time singing and meditating on the banks of the Kaveri River, deeply immersed in thoughts of Lord Ranganatha.

Miracles and Spiritual Experiences: A significant miracle in his life occurred when Lord Ranganatha himself commanded the temple priest, Loka Saranga, to carry Thiruppaan into the temple for darshan. Despite societal norms, Thiruppaan was lifted and taken into the sanctum, where he composed hymns upon seeing the Lord's divine form, eventually merging into the Lord's feet.

Notable Works: Amalan Adhipiraan, a set of 10 verses, is remarkable for its vivid description of Lord Ranganatha's beauty, from His feet to His crown, and expresses the joy and ecstasy of having seen the divine.

12. Thirumangai Azhwar (circa 8th–9th century CE)

Avatar of Vishnu: Sharanga (Vishnu's bow)

Birth and Early Life: Thirumangai Azhwar was born in Thirukurayalur and is believed to be an incarnation of Vishnu's bow, Sharnga. He initially led a life as a warrior and ruler of a small chieftaincy. His life changed drastically after a divine intervention that led him to become a passionate devotee of Lord Vishnu.

Miracles and Lesser-known Stories: Thirumangai Azhwar had a colorful life before his spiritual transformation. It is said that after his spiritual awakening, he led a band of robbers and even once robbed the temple jewels of Lord Ranganatha. However, the Lord revealed Himself to Thirumangai, leading to his repentance and complete surrender. He also constructed many temples and helped spread the Vaishnava tradition.

Notable Works: His works include Periya Thirumozhi, Thiruvezhukootrirukkai, and Thirukkurunthandagam, all of which are characterized by intense passion and devotion, expressing his love for Vishnu and his journey from sinner to saint.

The Azhwars' contributions go beyond mere devotional hymns. They revolutionized the religious landscape of South India, emphasizing personal devotion (bhakti) over ritualistic practices. Their hymns, which form the *Nalayira Divya Prabandham,* are still sung in Vishnu temples across Tamil Nadu, especially in the 108 *Divya Desams.* These saints also serve as role models for devotees, showing that God's grace is accessible to all, regardless of social status or birth. Through their lives, miracles, and hymns, the *Azhwars* continue to inspire devotion, compassion, and love for the divine.

Srivilliputhur

Srivilliputhur is a town in Tamil Nadu that embodies the timeless beauty and old-world charm of South India. It is a place where tradition, history, and spirituality blend harmoniously. Walking through its streets feels like stepping back in time, as the past continues to live on through its ancient temples, narrow streets, and simple yet deeply spiritual way of life.

At the heart of this town stands the magnificent Srivilliputhur Andal Temple, with its towering gopuram (gateway tower) that reaches the sky, intricately carved with mythological figures, gods, and celestial beings. This temple is not just a place of worship but the very soul of the town, drawing devotees from near and far. The streets surrounding the temple are lined with old-style houses, many with traditional courtyards and tiled roofs that have witnessed centuries pass by.

As you wander through the town's streets, you'll often encounter small, bustling markets where vendors sell garlands of fresh flowers, offerings for the temple, and a variety of local sweets and snacks. The scent of jasmine and incense fills the air, mingling with the sounds of temple bells and devotional hymns. There's a quiet rhythm to life here, one that revolves around the daily rituals of the temple, agricultural cycles, and the festivals that bring the entire town together.

Srivilliputhur's charm also lies in its simplicity. Life here moves at a slower pace, untouched by the rush of modernity.

You'll find craftsmen and artisans practicing age-old trades passed down through generations, such as weaving garlands, creating traditional handloom textiles, or crafting temple jewelry. The people are warm and welcoming, holding onto their customs and faith with a sense of pride.

The town is also surrounded by natural beauty. The rolling hills of the Western Ghats form a scenic backdrop, and lush groves of coconut, mango, and palm trees stretch across the landscape. During the monsoon, the area turns vibrant with greenery, and the sound of flowing water from nearby rivers adds to the serene atmosphere.

In the evenings, as the sun sets and the sky turns a deep shade of orange, the temple comes alive with the soft glow of oil lamps, and the air is filled with the chants of prayers. It is in these moments that you truly feel the spiritual energy that envelops the town, where the divine seems to be just within reach.

Srivilliputhur is not just a town; it's a living testament to Tamil Nadu's rich cultural heritage. Here, the ancient and sacred continue to thrive, offering visitors a glimpse into a life steeped in devotion, beauty, and peace. It is a place where devotion is woven into every aspect of life, where the divine feels close enough to touch, and where the air itself seems to hum with the prayers and blessings of centuries past. It's a town that invites you to slow down, to breathe deeply, and to feel the presence of the divine in every moment.

Srivilliputhur holds a special place in Tamil Nadu's identity, not just for its spiritual significance but also as a symbol of the state itself. The official emblem of Tamil Nadu prominently features an iconic image from Srivilliputhur – the towering Gopuram (temple tower) of the Srivilliputhur Andal Temple. This Gopuram is a central element of the state's emblem, representing Tamil Nadu's rich cultural and architectural heritage.

The emblem consists of the Lion Capital of Ashoka, symbolizing strength and justice, without the usual bell lotus foundation. This Lion Capital is flanked on either side by the Indian national flag, representing unity and the nation's pride. Behind the Lion Capital stands the image of the Srivilliputhur Andal Temple Gopuram, embodying the state's devotion, tradition, and its deep connection to its ancient temples.

Srivilliputhur is also renowned for its delectable milk sweet, Srivilliputhur Palkova. This traditional sweet is a must-try for anyone visiting the town. Made from locally sourced, pure milk that is slow-cooked and thickened with sugar, Palkova is known for its rich, creamy texture and melt-in-the-mouth taste. It is prepared following a time-honored recipe passed down through generations, making it an iconic treat synonymous with the town itself.

Vendors around the temple and the local markets sell freshly made Palkova, wrapped in banana leaves or packed in small containers, making it a popular offering for both the deities and visiting devotees. Its fame has spread far beyond Srivilliputhur, and the town has come to be known not just for its spiritual significance but also for this delicious, indulgent sweet that reflects the warmth and simplicity of the place.

Srivilliputhur is known not only for its rich cultural heritage and spiritual significance but also for its natural beauty, and it is home to the Srivilliputhur Grizzled Squirrel Wildlife Sanctuary. Nestled in the foothills of the Western Ghats, this sanctuary is a hidden gem for nature lovers and wildlife enthusiasts alike.

Established primarily to protect the endangered Grizzled Giant Squirrel, the sanctuary is a haven for a variety of wildlife species, including leopards, elephants, spotted deer, and a rich diversity of birds, making it a paradise for birdwatchers. The dense forests, rolling hills, and flowing streams within the sanctuary provide a serene and untouched landscape, offering a peaceful retreat into nature.

Trekking through the sanctuary, visitors can immerse themselves in the region's lush greenery while keeping an eye out for the elusive Grizzled Giant Squirrel and other wildlife that thrive in this protected area. The sanctuary preserves the region's natural habitat and adds to the charm of Srivilliputhur, where spirituality, culture, and nature come together in perfect harmony.

In addition to its spiritual heritage and natural beauty, Srivilliputhur is known for the majestic Sathuragiri Hills, a sacred and mystical mountain range. Often referred to as the "Abode of Gods," these hills hold great significance for pilgrims and trekkers, drawing those seeking adventure and spiritual fulfillment.

The name *Sathuragiri* is derived from two Tamil words: *Sathura*, meaning square, and *Giri*, meaning hill. The range is believed to resemble a square-shaped hill formation. According to local legends, this mystical mountain range is where the Siddhars - ancient sages who mastered the art of healing, spirituality, and the secrets of the universe - still reside in their subtle form, practicing divine worship and meditation.

Pilgrims often visit the Sundara Mahalingam Temple and the Santhana Mahalingam Temple, two ancient Shiva temples deep in the hills. These temples are considered highly sacred, and visiting them is seen as a journey of physical endurance and spiritual purification. The trek to *Sathuragiri* is challenging and rewarding. Steep paths and rugged terrain test visitors' stamina, while the breathtaking natural surroundings provide a sense of awe and tranquility.

The hills are also rich in medicinal plants, and the Siddhars reportedly used these rare herbs in their mystical healing practices. With their serene waterfalls, dense forests, and spiritually charged atmosphere, *Sathuragiri* Hills offers a perfect blend of nature, adventure, and devotion, making them a must-visit for anyone coming to Srivilliputhur.

The combination of the sacred Srivilliputhur Andal Temple, the scenic Srivilliputhur Grizzled Squirrel Wildlife Sanctuary, and the spiritual *Sathuragiri* Hills makes Srivilliputhur a destination that captivates both the heart and soul, leaving visitors with a deep sense of peace and wonder.

www.ingramcontent.com/pod-product-compliance
Lightning Source LLC
LaVergne TN
LVHW091307150826
845673LV00006B/1563
9798895889077